Miniature BALTIMORE ALBUM *Quilts*

Jenifer Buechel

That Patchwork Place®

Dedication

In loving memory of my mother, Shirley Carpenter, who taught me to appreciate
all the needle arts—none of which are worth doing unless done right—and who
wouldn't believe that this is what I have dedicated my life to.

Acknowledgments

First, a special thank-you to my students. Without their participation and encouragement, this book would be much less than complete.

To Karen Mongomery and Mary Beth Harnett, two special quilt-shop owners who patiently listened and reassured me throughout the process, thank you for all your help.

To Vivian Dibrell, Polly Marsh, Nancy Howard, Bernice Croushore, Mabel Riley, Marilyn Ingalls, Janine Franc, Marion Ludwig, and Sue Lazaroff, thank you for allowing me to display your beautiful quilts in this book. They are truly wonderful!

To Elly Sienkiewicz and Judith Montano, two talented teachers, thank you for your inspiration and encouragement.

To Nancy Howard and Kathy Oppelt, thank you for your long-distance help and encouragement. I miss not being closer.

To Brenda White, thank you for the last-minute stitching. It helped tremendously.

To everyone at That Patchwork Place, thank you for this opportunity and for your support throughout this project.

To Ron, Heather, and Ryan, my family, thank you for tying up the computer at inopportune times. Seriously, thank you for putting up with being neglected by me and for supporting me. (Heather, I will try to wake up on time now.)

To Annie Tuley, who "sewed" the seed for this whole project, thanks so much. Your ideas and creativity are woven through the silk ribbons. I can't wait to present you with your quilt. By the way, what brilliant ideas do you have now?

Lastly, a very special thank-you to my "quarter-century" friend, Joy. Without your daily company and talks, I just wouldn't be me. Thanks for your unwavering support, gentle nudges of encouragement, and generous help, and for making life in general so much better. Love ya, "Sis."

Credits

Editor-in-Chief: Kerry I. Hoffman
Technical Editor: Melissa A. Lowe
Managing Editor: Judy Petry
Design Director: Cheryl Stevenson
Copy Editor: Liz McGehee
Proofreader: Melissa Riesland
Illustrator: Laurel Strand
Illustration Assistants: Bruce Stout, Robin Strobel
Photographer: Brent Kane
Text and Cover Designer: Amy Shayne
Production Assistant: Claudia L'Heureux

MISSION STATEMENT

WE ARE DEDICATED TO PROVIDING QUALITY
PRODUCTS AND SERVICES THAT INSPIRE CREATIVITY.
WE WORK TOGETHER TO ENRICH THE LIVES WE TOUCH.
That Patchwork Place is a financially responsible ESOP company.

Miniature Baltimore Album Quilts
© 1997 by Jenifer Buechel
That Patchwork Place, Inc.
PO Box 118, Bothell, WA 98041-0118 USA

Library of Congress Cataloging-in-Publication Data
Buechel, Jenifer,
    Miniature Baltimore album quilts / Jenifer Buechel.
        p.   cm.
    Includes bibliographical references.
    ISBN 1-56477-176-8
    1. Patchwork—Patterns. 2. Appliqué—Patterns. 3. Album quilts.
4. Miniature quilts. I. Title.
TT835.B783   1997   96-30983
746.46'041—dc20   CIP

Printed in Hong Kong
01 00 99 98 97 96   6 5 4 3 2 1

CONTENTS

INTRODUCTION

While writing this book, I thought about the path that led to the Miniature Baltimore Album quilt. My love for traditional Baltimore Album quilts is probably what started it. I have designed and started many Baltimore Album–style quilts, but this one was special—I finished it.

I love learning new needlework techniques, and I try to incorporate as many of these techniques as I can into my quilts and classes. When I was introduced to silk-ribbon embroidery, I was instantly fascinated. As I planned projects for silk-ribbon embroidery classes, a friend of mine innocently suggested that I combine the technique with Baltimore Album blocks. She thought the dimensional flowers and leaves would be ideal for a miniature Baltimore Album basket. This blossomed from a small, four-block project into a sixteen-month class, my miniature replica of a Baltimore Album–style quilt, a hand-dyed silk-ribbon business, and this book. I have a feeling I'm not done yet.

HISTORY

Baltimore Album–style quilts are based on ornately appliquéd quilts made in the Baltimore, Maryland, area in the mid-1800s. These quilts feature baskets and vases overflowing with flowers; wreaths of roses, acorns, and strawberries; folk art–style red-and-green quilt blocks; and ornate picture blocks. Most of the antique Baltimore Album quilts seem to be the combined effort of many women donating appliquéd blocks to commemorate a special occasion or to honor a certain person. Delicate inked signatures may indicate the stitcher or donor of a particular block. The artists often included special sayings or remembrances, embellished with scrolls and garlands, for the lucky recipient of such a gift.

Antique Baltimore Album quilts share certain themes and Victorian-era symbols. Bouquets were artfully arranged using the language of flowers, similar to the way a Victorian lady would arrange a bouquet of real flowers. White roses, representing purity and grace, were often a prominent part of a block design. A red book or album may have been modeled after popular album books, inside which a Victorian lady kept cherished mementos. Eagle designs displayed a lady's patriotism, while other birds and small animals showed her love of nature. Monuments, manor houses, and ships were often focal points, meant to commemorate special events or areas of interest in the city of Baltimore. Close inspection of the block designs reveals something special about each artist.

All types of fabrics, including cotton, velvet, silk, and wool, were used in Baltimore Album quilts. Many of these quilts include dimensional techniques, such as stuffed flower petals and grapes, ruched roses, and embroidered accents on leaves and buds. I have found no mention of silk-ribbon embroidery in my study of antique Baltimore Album quilts, although it was in practice at the time. I have found several references to ornamental needlework, which includes silk-ribbon embroidery. Typically, these were projects for teaching young women advanced needlework. The examples I have seen are amazingly similar in style to Baltimore Album blocks.

There are a number of books on antique Baltimore Album quilts, Baltimore Album–style quilts, and silk-ribbon embroidery. (See "Bibliography" on page 95.) You may want to look at these books to learn more about traditional block designs and color usage. In creating my miniature block designs, I tried to honor the original Baltimore Album designs, incorporating many of the techniques as well as the style of these quilts.

GETTING STARTED

Please read the instructions carefully before you begin. I have included many tips and suggestions that make creating your Miniature Baltimore Album quilt easier. You will need twenty-five blocks for a Miniature Baltimore Album quilt, or use fewer blocks for a small quilt. There are twenty-eight block patterns (pages 52–84) and three border patterns (pages 92–94) from which to choose. I encourage you to have fun and be creative. For ideas, look at the quilts on pages 13–20.

Start by gathering your materials and supplies for one block, then follow the step-by-step directions for constructing (pages 10–12) and embroidering (pages 21–35) the block. Repeat these steps for each block. To complete your quilt, follow the directions for assembling and finishing the quilt (pages 85–91).

Materials

Because there are so many options and possibilities, a Miniature Baltimore Album quilt is a wonderful opportunity to work with different materials and express your creativity. As a teacher, I find a lot of people are intimidated by too many choices. Start by focusing on just one or two blocks rather than the entire quilt. Above all, have fun with these materials and designs.

FUSIBLE WEB

The embroidery in these blocks is strictly decorative; the appliqué pieces are fused rather than stitched to the background fabric. One yard of lightweight, paper-backed fusible web is probably more than enough to make an entire Miniature Baltimore Album quilt. *Don't try to use up old paper-backed fusible web in these blocks.* Older paper-backed fusible web doesn't seem to bond as well. Because the embroidery is decorative, the bond between the appliqué and the background fabric is very important.

FABRIC

I recommend using good-quality, tightly woven 100% cotton fabric for your Miniature Baltimore Album quilt. All measurements in this book are based on 44"-wide fabric.

It is important to prewash the fabric in warm water, with or without detergent, to remove the manufacturer's sizing and to test for colorfastness. Sizing may prevent fusible web from bonding with the fabric. Following the wash cycle, check the rinse water for excess dye (colored water). Repeat the rinse cycle twice. If you still see excess dye in the rinse water, do not use that fabric. It will only cause you problems.

Background Fabric

In antique Baltimore Album quilts, the background fabric is usually solid white or off-white. Today, we have more options. Many of the quilts in this book have wonderful tone-on-tone print background fabrics. Try a black or dark-colored background; I think this would be stunning. As you make your fabric choices, remember that the color and value of the background will influence the colors and values of the appliqué fabric, thread, and silk ribbon. These should complement rather than compete with the background fabric.

If you decide to use a print for the background fabric, I recommend a subtle pattern. A large or obvious pattern will detract from the delicacy of the miniature blocks. Also, some fabrics are printed with a heavy ink that sits on top of the fabric. (If you rub the fabric between your fingers, you can feel this ink.) These fabrics can be difficult to hand stitch.

You need a 6" x 6" square of background fabric for each block and enough yardage for a matching border if desired. To make all twenty-five blocks and a matching border, you need about 1½ yards of background fabric.

This is also a good time to think about backing fabric. You may want to use the same fabric for the background, border, and backing. In this case, you need 2½ yards of fabric. It is much easier to purchase the backing fabric at the same time as the background and border fabric than to decide you want the same fabric later, when it is no longer available. (I have spent many a day chasing around to quilt stores for this very reason.) To estimate the yardage needed to bind the quilt, see "Binding" on pages 90–91.

It is usually better to have the same or a lighter shade of backing fabric. Dark-colored backing fabric may show through to the front of a light-colored quilt. Test your choices by laying the background fabric on top of the backing fabric to see if it shows through.

Appliqué Fabric

Baltimore Album quilts traditionally share a common color scheme: turkey red, dark green, royal blue, and deep gold. You can study antique Baltimore Album quilts for ideas or create your own palette. Remember, the original Baltimore Album quilts were often created by different artists with different sewing skills, color preferences, and design ideas. Look at the "Gallery of Quilts" (pages 13–20) for color and fabric ideas.

Small-scale or "mini" prints are ideal for the appliqué pieces, but don't rule out large-scale prints. Sometimes the colors and shading in a large-scale print are perfect, especially if you don't want a tiny pattern to become the focus. Textured and tone-on-tone prints are wonderful for appliquéd leaves.

Finally, you can use specialty fabrics, such as lamé and satin, instead of 100% cotton for your appliqué pieces. Be aware, though, that specialty fabrics need special attention. These fabrics may fray, discolor from the heat of the iron, and cause general mayhem. But if you have your heart set on using a particular fabric, give it a try. It may provide just the spark you were looking for. For best results, test the specialty fabric to see if it will fuse to the background fabric, and don't use fabric that is a heavier weight than cotton. Most important, have fun choosing your fabric!

THREAD

Select your thread after you fuse the appliqué pieces to the background squares. As a general rule, choose a lighter or darker value of the same color used for the appliqué piece. For example, if you are embroidering green leaves, choose a shade of green thread lighter or darker than the leaves. The shade of thread will complement the color of the appliqué pieces.

In some blocks, thread or braid is an important part of the design. On an urn or vase, for example, you may want to outline certain areas with a contrasting or completely different color of thread or braid. As you plan each block, decide whether you want to accent certain parts of the design.

Two strands of embroidery floss or an equivalent-weight thread highlight without overwhelming the appliqué pieces. This is a great excuse to try the many wonderful threads available. Don't limit yourself to embroidery floss; experiment with all types of threads.

Embroidery floss: Six-strand cotton embroidery floss, such as DMC®, is readily available and comes in a multitude of colors. Cross-stitchers "strip" the floss (separate the strands), then thread the number of strands they need onto a needle. Stripping makes the floss easier to control; it also gives you the option of using two colors at the same time, creating the illusion of another color.

Single-strand cotton floss is also available. This has a different look than six-strand embroidery floss, with a matte rather than shiny finish. Single-strand cotton floss is usually equivalent to two strands of embroidery floss. Single-strand floss may fray and shred as you stitch; for best results, work with 12"-long pieces.

Metallic threads, blending filaments, and rayon threads: These threads add a delightful sparkle to your blocks. Use them alone or combine them with one strand of embroidery floss. Make sure you use an embroidery needle with an eye large enough to accommodate these threads. Some metallic threads tend to snag on the fabric weave as you stitch. If you use a slightly larger embroidery needle (which makes a bigger hole in the fabric), you will have less trouble.

Silk buttonhole twist: This is a wonderful thread with a lovely sheen. It is slightly thicker than two strands of embroidery floss and may be a little more difficult to work with, but it is well worth the effort. I wax this thread with beeswax to make it easier to control.

Silk floss: While silk floss is not as easy to find as embroidery floss, it can be a real treat to work with. For best results, use a 12"-long piece and wax the strands.

Wool thread: This was often used to buttonhole stitch around appliqués in antique Baltimore Album quilts. You can duplicate this look with wool and wool-blend thread. Wool thread, available in a wide range of colors, adds a unique texture and look. Like cotton floss, wool thread may fray and shred as you stitch. For best results, work with 12"-long pieces.

TIMESAVING TIP

It is a good idea to jot in a notebook the color numbers for the embroidery floss and silk ribbon you've chosen. It is much easier to find a color when you know the number than to try and match a swatch or recall the correct color.

SILK RIBBON

Silk ribbon has become the popular choice for most ribbon-embroidery projects. Its softness and drapability make it perfect for creating dimensional flowers and leaves. Silk ribbon is usually available at local fabric, quilting, and craft stores, as well as through mail-order suppliers. Read the package labels. There is a synthetic silk ribbon that is slightly cheaper than genuine silk ribbon. You can use the synthetic in place of real silk ribbon, but it may be more difficult to work with.

Silk ribbon is available in different widths: 2mm, 4mm, 7mm, 13mm, and wider. The blocks in this book are scaled for 4mm ribbon, the most readily available size.

Begin with a few colors and work your way through several blocks before investing in a lot of silk ribbon. Look at the "Gallery of Quilts" (pages 13–20) for color ideas. Use variegated or hand-dyed silk ribbon, which has different colors or different shades of one color on the same ribbon, to create multicolored or more realistic flowers, fruit, and foliage. The variations in color and shading add a dimension to silk-ribbon embroidery that solid colors cannot.

It's hard to estimate how much ribbon you will need because everyone applies a different amount of tension as they stitch. As a rule of thumb, you will need 12" of silk ribbon for each rose or flower. (Silk ribbon frays and tears easily, so work with 12" lengths.)

The size 18 chenille needle works well for silk-ribbon embroidery, but try different sizes until you find one that is comfortable for you. Keep in mind, the larger the needle, the bigger the hole it will make in the fabric, and the less wear and tear on the ribbon.

If your silk ribbon is wrinkled or creased, use a curling iron to press it. Just clip the ribbon in the curling iron and draw it through for perfectly ironed ribbon.

SAVING AND STORING SILK RIBBON

Save leftover pieces of silk ribbon, 3" or longer, for buds and tiny accent flowers. I keep a small plastic zipper-type bag handy for storing these pieces.

Coloring Your Own Silk Ribbon

You can purchase variegated or hand-dyed silk ribbon (see "Resources" on page 95), or create your own. I've included instructions for silk paint, which is safer and easier to use than silk dye. Always follow the manufacturer's instructions and safety precautions for using paint or dye.

Using Silk Paint

Silk and fabric paints both contain pigment in a gluelike base. This base bonds the pigment to the fiber, slightly stiffening the ribbon or fabric. For lighter values, thin the paint with water. Experiment with blending paints to create new colors.

1. Cut silk ribbon into 12"-long pieces.
2. Dampen the ribbon with water.
3. Using a small paintbrush, paint the ribbon.
4. Preheat your iron to a silk setting, then iron the ribbon until dry to set the paint. Be sure to test for colorfastness. (See "Testing for Colorfastness" on page 8.)

Using Silk Dye

Unlike silk paint, silk dye does not affect the feel of the ribbon because the molecules in the dye actually form a chemical bond with the silk fiber. Any silk dye will work, as long as the ribbon is 100% silk.

Silk dye must be steam-set or dipped in a chemical fixative to be colorfast. Follow the manufacturer's instructions and safety precautions.

BRAID

The Beaded Basket (page 56) and Traditional Red Basket (page 79) blocks are woven with ⅛"-wide rayon braid. The Woven Basket block (page 83) features Bunka rayon cording, which is available in a variety of colors and can be threaded on a needle. The Blooming Basket block (page 60) includes narow upholstery gimp. See the block patterns for more information on these braids.

Braids are often used by miniaturists and dollmakers to trim doll clothes and are available at fabric or craft stores, at dollmaking-supply stores, and through mail-order suppliers. (See "Resources" on page 95.) Most braids are colorfast, but always check to make sure.

Testing for Colorfastness

Unless you are never going to wash the blocks or quilt, test the colorfastness of your fabric, thread, silk ribbon, and braid. It's better to be safe than sorry! (Refer to page 5 for instructions on testing fabric.) To test thread, silk ribbon, or braid, wet a small piece and pat it dry with a white paper towel. If you see any dye or color on the paper towel, it is not colorfast. Purple and deep shades of red are the worst culprits.

You can try to rinse out excess dye by soaking the thread, silk ribbon, or braid in warm water, changing the water until it stays clear; or try setting the dye as described below.

1. *Combine ¼ cup vinegar, ¾ cup warm water, and a ¼ teaspoon salt in a glass measuring cup.*
2. *Gently swish the thread, silk ribbon, or braid around in the solution. If the water remains clear, you should be able to use it. If the dye bleeds, repeat the process until the water stays clear.*
3. *Air-dry and iron as necessary.*

BEADS

Small beads add just the right sparkle to baskets, urns, and clusters of grapes, and as silk-ribbon flower centers. Craft and fabric stores carry a wide array of beads. The beads used to decorate cross-stitch projects are the perfect size for these blocks, or you may want to use larger or different-shaped beads for accents, such as the spider on Bernice Croushore's quilt "Remember Me" (page 13) or the bugle beads embellishing the urn on Nancy Howard's "With Love and Flowers Too" (page 17).

Use strong quilting thread for beading. Choose a color that blends with the background fabric or ribbon, not the bead. You can also purchase special beading thread. This is a wonderfully strong, waxed nylon that reminds me of dental floss. It is available in white or black; choose the color that best blends with the background.

BATTING

Once you've assembled the quilt top, you will need batting. For best results, use a low-loft batting. The batting size depends on the size of your quilt top. I generally recommend cutting the batting 1" to 3" larger than the quilt top on all sides. Measure your quilt top to determine the size needed.

Tools

ROTARY-CUTTING EQUIPMENT

You need a rotary cutter, cutting guide, and self-healing mat for cutting the background squares and border strips, and for trimming the finished blocks. These tools make cutting and trimming faster and easier. If you prefer, use a pair of fabric scissors.

EMBROIDERY SCISSORS

A pair of sharp embroidery scissors is essential. These blocks feature tiny and detailed appliqués. The smaller and sharper your scissors, the easier it is to cut the appliqué pieces.

NEEDLES

You need several different types of needles to make a Miniature Baltimore Album quilt. If you are new to embroidery, choose a package of needles that includes an assortment of sizes. Experiment with different sizes until you find a needle you feel comfortable using. As general rule, the smaller the needle, the smaller the stitch you can make.

Appliqué (Sharp): Use appliqué needles or Sharps to tack or gather the silk ribbon. I also use these needles for beading. Appliqués or Sharps are thin enough to pass through the beads and don't bend like beading needles.

Chenille: The size 18 chenille needle works well for silk-ribbon embroidery. The tight weave of cotton fabric can stress silk ribbon. Avoid this by using a large needle, such as a chenille. Because this size needle makes a bigger hole in the fabric, the ribbon is less likely to fray or shred as you stitch.

Embroidery: I like to use a size 8 embroidery needle. It is a small embroidery needle, but the eye is large enough for two strands of floss or decorative thread.

Quilting: Commonly referred to as "Betweens," these small needles are perfect for fine hand quilting. The smaller the needle, the smaller the stitches. If you are a beginning quilter, try a size 10.

Tapestry: These needles work well for woven-ribbon embroidery and can be used for silk-ribbon embroidery. While the blunt point won't snag the ribbon, it is much harder to push through the cotton fabric. A size 22 works well.

MARKING PENCILS

Use water-soluble marking pencils, such as dressmakers' chalk, to transfer block designs to your background fabric. Be sure to use marking pencils that wash out. Wax-based marking pencils may set when you iron the appliqués to your background fabric. If so, you won't be able to wash the marks out. For best results, test each marking pencil on scraps before using it in your projects.

Use a lead pencil or permanent-ink black marker to trace block designs on paper-backed fusible web.

OPTIONAL TOOLS

An embroidery hoop is optional. Try working with and without a hoop to see which works best for you. One advantage of working with a hoop is it eliminates puckering in the background fabric. (If you choose to work without a hoop, you can remedy puckering by blocking your quilt blocks as described on page 85.) One disadvantage of working with a hoop is that some silk-ribbon and embroidery stitches are more awkward.

A thimble is also optional. I refuse to quilt without a thimble, but I don't use one while doing embroidery.

On a few blocks, you may need to stitch through the appliqué piece, fusible web, and background fabric, which can be challenging. Try using an awl to make a small hole in the fabric before stitching; this makes it easier to pull thread and ribbon through the fabric.

If you have an appliqué piece that won't stay in place after fusing, try using a bit of permanent-bond fabric glue.

WORKING WITH AN EMBROIDERY HOOP

To make your block fit a standard embroidery hoop, baste 3"-wide strips of scrap fabric around your 6" square of background fabric.

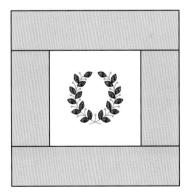

CONSTRUCTING THE BLOCKS

To make a Miniature Baltimore Album quilt, you need twenty-five blocks. This book includes patterns for twenty-eight different blocks. You do not need to choose in advance which quilt blocks to include—just work one block at a time.

Cutting Background Fabric

Each block finishes to 4" x 4". I recommend working on a larger square of background fabric, 6" x 6", then trimming it to 4½" x 4½" before assembling the quilt top. This approach allows you to adjust the block size (there will be some shrinkage from stitching) and to make sure the pattern is centered.

Before you cut your blocks, be sure to prewash your fabric and test for colorfastness as described on page 5. Iron your fabric before cutting.

1. Cut four 6"-wide strips from background fabric.
2. Trim the selvage edges, then cut the strips into 6" squares. You should have 28 squares. Save the remaining background fabric for the borders.

If you don't have a rotary cutter, use a marking pencil and ruler to mark a grid of 6" blocks on the fabric. Use fabric scissors to cut out the blocks.

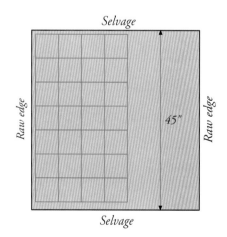

If you are using scissors, mark a grid of 6" squares before cutting.

Tracing the Block Patterns

You will need one 6" square of background fabric for each block, pins or tape, and a water-soluble marking pencil. Test your marking pencil before you begin to make sure it will wash out.

1. Fold a square of background fabric into quarters and finger-press the folds to make a grid.
2. Using the grid, center the fabric square on the placement guide. Pin or tape the placement guide and fabric so they will not shift as you work.
3. Referring to the Placement and Embroidery Guide with each block pattern, mark 1 small dot for each outside corner of the block, then trace the placement guide.

If you cannot see the placement guide through your fabric, use a window or light table to help transfer the pattern. Tape the pattern and fabric on a sunny window. (I've even used the TV screen in a pinch.) To make a light table, place a piece of glass between the leaves of a table, then position a lamp underneath.

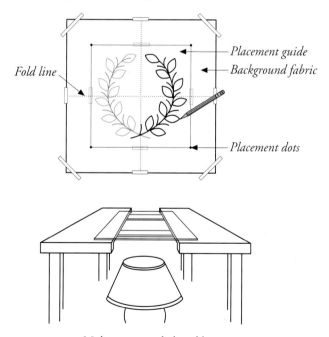

Make your own light table.

Signing Your Blocks

Many antique Baltimore Album quilts feature blocks with lovely signatures, sayings, and small artistic motifs. Imitate this idea by adding your name and the date to a wreath block or by creating a special block with a banner or border design. If you are not artistically inclined, check the library, bookstore, and art- or craft-supply store for clip-art books with Victorian designs. As you think about designs, remember that these are miniature blocks. It may be hard to draw or trace a design with a lot of detail. You may want to have a design resized at the copy shop so it will fit the quilt block.

I recommend using a Pigma™ pen to draw on your blocks. Pigma pens are available in various tip sizes and ink colors. For the finest line, use a .005 size Pigma pen. This size is well suited for small, delicate artwork. You can also create an illusion of shading by going over some of the design lines more than once. Always test the pen on a scrap of background fabric to be sure it does not bleed. Sometimes applying a spray sizing—not starch—to the back of the fabric will help control the ink and make the fabric easier to write on. For best results, use a light touch and practice on a fabric scrap before writing on your block.

Many people are hesitant to write on a quilt. It is relatively painless, especially if you practice first. One of the best ways to avoid a mistake is to draw or trace the complete design on paper, then trace the design onto the background fabric. Or trace the block pattern as described above, then add your signature or saying. Always add your remembrance before fusing the appliqué pieces. (If you make a mistake, you won't ruin a finished block.) As you fuse the appliqué pieces to the background fabric, the heat will set the ink in the fabric.

Tracing and Fusing the Appliqués

You will need appliqué fabric for each block, paper-backed fusible web, a lead pencil or permanent-ink black marker, an iron and ironing surface, small embroidery scissors, tweezers or pins, and background fabric. To reduce the chance of mixing pieces from different blocks, trace and fuse appliqué pieces for one block at a time. Note that some appliqué pieces are reversed for you.

Always trace the appliqué patterns on the paper side of the fusible web. (The fusible-web side feels slightly nubby, while the paper side is smooth.) Follow these steps for all the block patterns.

1. Using a lead pencil or permanent-ink marker, trace all the appliqué pieces onto the paper side of the fusible web. I like to group the appliqué pieces that are the same or are going to be fused onto the same fabric in a section, rather than trace the appliqué pattern directly onto the fusible web. For example, look at the Roses with a Peacock block on page 76. First, I traced all the leaves onto one section of the fusible web, then I traced the branches, bird body, and wing in other sections.

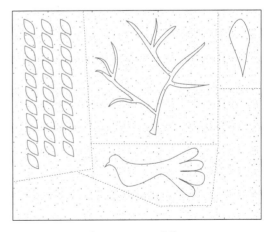

Group appliqué pieces in different sections.

2. Cut the groups of appliqué pieces apart. Referring to the manufacturer's instructions, fuse a section to the wrong side of the appliqué fabric. Repeat for each section.

3. Using a pair of small embroidery scissors, cut out the appliqué pieces. If you are working with an appliqué piece that has small open areas, such as the loops in a bow, remove these before cutting out the appliqué piece.

4. Working as gently as possible, peel the paper backing from the appliqués. The edges of the appliqué pieces will fray easily, and the pieces may not fuse correctly. If you have a hard time peeling the paper from the appliqué pieces, try using tweezers, or score the center of the paper with a pin (this cuts the paper, but not the fabric), then fold the appliqué in half along the score line and grab a loose end of paper to peel off.

5. Following the placement guide, fuse the appliqué pieces to the background square. Make sure the pieces are securely fused to the background fabric. The decorative stitching around these appliqués is not going to hold them in place. Use fabric glue for stray appliqué pieces only as a last resort and for an occasional appliqué piece, not the whole quilt.

POSITIONING APPLIQUÉ PIECES

I like to sit at my ironing board so I can position the pieces and press. This keeps the appliqué pieces from shifting during a trip to the ironing board. Use a pair of tweezers to accurately place small pieces.

GALLERY OF QUILTS

Remember Me
by Bernice Croushore, 1995, White
Oak, Pennsylvania, 26" x 26".
Bernice's sewing block makes this
Album quilt very special. Note the
spiderweb embroidered into the
grapevine border.

Joy
by Marion Ludwig, 1995,
Pittsburgh, Pennsylvania, 26" x 26".

Return of the Grapevine Wreath
by Jenifer Buechel, 1996, Pittsburgh,
Pennsylvania, 16" x 16".
Quilted by Joy Mays.

Baltimore Feathers
by Jenifer Buechel, 1996,
Pittsburgh, Pennsylvania, 22" x 22".
Quilted by Joy Mays.

Medley of Ribbons for Sarah
by Marilyn Ingalls, 1995, Upper
Saint Clair, Pennsylvania, 25" x 25".
Marilyn's granddaughter Sarah
watched her make this quilt, so
Marilyn dedicated it to her.

Mini Baltimore Album
by Polly Marsh, 1995,
Pittsburgh, Pennsylvania,
26" x 26". Polly's workmanship
is phenomenal.

With Love and Flowers Too
by Nancy Howard, 1995,
Cambridge, Massachusetts,
33" x 33". Sashing sets each block
apart. The meandering border is an
attractive frame for this quilt.

Lest We Forget
by Mabel Riley, 1995, McKeesport, Pennsylvania, 26" x 26". This color scheme has a Southwestern flavor. The teal, peach, and mauve give this quilt its own personality.

Roland Avenue Memories
by Vivian Dibrell, 1995, Bethel Park, Pennsylvania, 30" x 30". This quilt has many additions and subtle changes.

Three Block Sampler
by Suzanne Lazaroff, 1995,
Pittsburgh, Pennsylvania, 11" x 19".
Sue could not resist making all
twenty-eight block designs in this
book. She set the remaining three
into a sampler.

Paint the Town
by Janine Franc, 1995, Pittsburgh,
Pennsylvania, 33" x 33". Janine's
color selections and two original
blocks make this Album quilt a
variation on the traditional.

Miniature Baltimore Album I
by Jenifer Buechel, 1995, Pittsburgh,
Pennsylvania, 26" x 26".

EMBROIDERING THE BLOCKS

This stitch guide includes embroidery stitches for outlining the appliqués, and silk-ribbon stitches for embellishing the blocks. If you have never done any embroidery, practice on a sample piece, then use this sampler as a guide when you need to review.

Refer to pages 6–7 for suggestions on embroidery floss, thread, and silk ribbon. Here are a few hints and reminders for embroidering Miniature Baltimore Album blocks:

❋ Outline all the appliqués with an embroidery stitch.

❋ Outline the appliqués before adding embellishments, such as silk-ribbon roses and beads. It's much easier to outline the appliqué pieces before you add flowers than to embroider around the flowers.

❋ Use two strands of embroidery floss or the equivalent in another type of thread to outline the appliqués.

❋ Focus on making neat, even embroidery stitches rather than small stitches. Granted, you would like small stitches, but your blocks will look much nicer if your stitches are neat and even.

❋ To prevent embroidery floss or thread from tangling or fraying as you stitch, use 12" to 18" lengths. I strongly recommend using 12" lengths when working with silk ribbon, which frays easily.

❋ If you have never worked with silk ribbon, practice on a sample piece before stitching your block. Use less tension with silk ribbon than you would with embroidery floss or thread. The flowers in silk-ribbon embroidery should look three-dimensional. Keep your stitches loose.

❋ If the instructions call for silk ribbon and matching thread, make sure you thread a needle of each before you begin stitching. It is much easier to have both handy than to set down a silk-ribbon flower to thread another needle.

❋ Keep an eye on the back of your block. There is nothing more frustrating than catching a stitch or knot on the back of the block and pulling out a previous stitch. Train yourself to feel the previous stitches so you can avoid this problem.

❋ Weave the ends of your embroidery floss through the stitches on the back of your block to keep the tails from shadowing through on the front.

Threading and Knotting Silk Ribbon

To save ribbon, thread and knot silk ribbon as described below.

1. *Thread one end of the ribbon through the eye of the needle.*
2. *Take the tip of the needle through one end of the ribbon.*

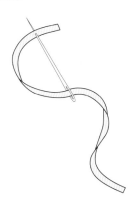

3. *Pull the ribbon until it locks on the eye.*
4. *To put a knot on the other end of the ribbon, take a stitch in and out of the ribbon.*

5. *Slide the stitch down the length of the ribbon; a knot will form at the end.*

Always end your stitching on the back of the block. Knot the ribbon onto another stitch (make sure you don't pull too tight and pucker your fabric) or cut off the ribbon, leaving a tail to be tacked down later with matching thread. The latter method works well with stitches that need matching thread. If you have more stitching, leave a tail and draw the next piece of ribbon through it. This locks the tail in place. Try to keep the back of your work as neat as possible to minimize shadowing on the front.

Stitches

BACKSTITCH

Use this stitch to outline the appliqués or as a foundation for the threaded backstitch (page 33).

1. Bring the needle up at point A and down at point B.
2. Bring the needle up again at point C and continue.

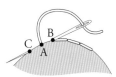

BULLION STITCH

Use this stitch to make a bullion rose (page 23), round bullion rose (page 31), or small rosebuds for filling areas in your blocks.

1. Bring the needle up at point A and down at point B. Bring the tip of the needle up again at point A, leaving it in the fabric, facing away from you.
2. Wrap embroidery floss or silk ribbon around the tip of the needle 5 to 8 times (depending on the length of the stitch between point A and point B). If you are using silk ribbon, keep the ribbon flat against the needle.
3. Gently pull the floss or ribbon through the wraps. (I like to use my thumb to hold the wraps on the needle as I pull the floss or ribbon through.) Bring the needle down at point B.
4. Gently tug on the floss or ribbon to make sure the wraps are evenly distributed along the stitch.

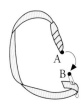

BULLION ROSE

Mark the position of the bullion on the block before you begin.

1. Make 6 bullions in the order shown below.
2. Make 3 lazy daisy stitches (page 29) at the base of the bullions.
3. Make 2 ribbon stitches (page 30) framing the bullions, using the same color of thread or ribbon as in step 2.

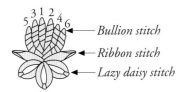

← Bullion stitch

← Ribbon stitch

← Lazy daisy stitch

BULLION-TIPPED DAISY

Use this stitch to make leaves and flower petals with a pointed tip.

1. Bring the needle up at point A and down again just in front of point A. Bring the tip of the needle up at point B, leaving the needle in the fabric.
2. Wrap the embroidery floss or silk ribbon around the needle 3 times. If you are using silk ribbon, keep the ribbon flat against the needle.
3. Gently pull the floss or ribbon through the wraps. (Use your thumb to hold the wraps on the needle as you pull the floss or ribbon through.) Bring the needle down at point C, just beyond the bullion tip at point B.

BULLION-TIPPED FLOWER

1. Following the instructions for a bullion-tipped daisy, make 4 to 6 flower petals.
2. Make a French knot (page 27) or stitch a small bead for the flower center.

BUTTONHOLE STITCH

This stitch works well for outlining appliqués.

1. Bring the needle up at point A, down at point B, then up again at point C.
2. Repeat. Stitch through the edge of the appliqué piece between points B and C.

BUTTONHOLE STITCH FLOWER

1. Work a buttonhole stitch in a circle, following the numbers as shown. Always bring the needle up close to the center.
2. Make a straight stitch for the last petal (#6).
3. Make French knots (page 27) or stitch small beads for the flower center.

CHAIN STITCH

This stitch works well for outlining appliqués and making chain stitch roses. When using this stitch to outline appliqués, be sure to keep your needle aligned with the edge of the appliqué.

1. Bring the needle up at point A, down just behind point A, then up at point B.
2. For the next stitch, bring the needle down just behind point B (inside the loop) and up at point C.
3. Repeat as desired. To finish, bring the needle to the back of the fabric, over the loop of the last chain.

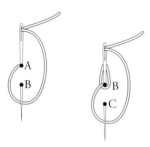

CORAL STITCH ROSE

For this stitch, keep the tension loose.

1. Make 3 French knots (page 27) for flower center.
2. Bring the needle up at point A, down at point B, and up at point C, wrapping the embroidery floss or silk ribbon over and under the needle.
3. Gently pull the floss or ribbon until a loose knot forms. (The loose knots form the petals of the rose.)
4. Continue stitching in a spiral, bringing the needle down at point D and up at point E, and wrapping the floss or ribbon over and under the needle.

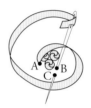

CHAIN STITCH ROSE

For a fuller flower, keep your stitches loose.

1. Make 3 French knots (page 27) for flower center.
2. Work a chain stitch in a spiral around the French knots until the rose is the desired size.

COUCH STITCH

Use a couch stitch to secure embroidery floss, thread, silk ribbon, or decorative cording (such as in the Woven Basket block on page 83). Thread a second needle with thread for this stitch.

1. Take a stitch with the floss, thread, ribbon, or cording you want to couch.
2. Bring the second needle up at point A (almost under the stitch made in step 1) and down at point B.
3. Repeat, spacing the couching stitches evenly along the length of the stitch made in step 1.

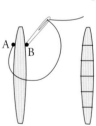

COUCHED LOOP FLOWER

Couch this looped flower with matching thread.

1. Make 3 to 5 French knots (page 27) for the flower center.
2. Thread a 12"-long piece of silk ribbon on one needle and a matching-colored thread on a second needle.
3. Bring both needles up at point A.
4. Form a loop of ribbon for the first petal.
5. With the matching thread, couch the ribbon petal, catching the edge of the ribbon at point B.
6. Bring the needle with the matching thread up again close to point A. Form another loop of ribbon and couch, catching the edge of the ribbon at point B.
7. Repeat until you have enough loops for your flower. Finish by knotting the ribbon and thread on the back of the block.

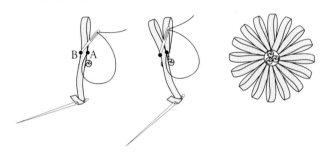

COUCHED RIBBON STEM

This stitch looks like thorns on a stem.

1. Thread one needle with a 12"-long piece of silk ribbon and a second needle with matching thread.
2. Using the first needle, make a straight stitch (page 33). Bring the needle up at point A and down at point B.
3. Bring the second needle up at point C and down at point D. Stitch at an angle, gently pulling the ribbon to the side. Repeat.

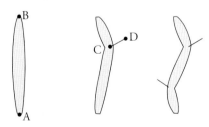

CROSS-STITCH FLOWER

Use this tiny flower as filler where you need a few small flowers.

1. Bring the needle up at point A, down at point B, then up at point C.
2. To finish the cross-stitch, bring the needle down at point D.
3. To make the center of the flower, couch the center with a second color of embroidery floss or silk ribbon, bringing the needle up at point E and down at point F.

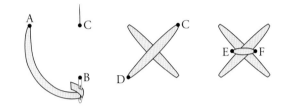

ELONGATED LAZY DAISY

Use this stitch to make rosebuds or leaves. Make a lazy daisy stitch (page 29), but elongate the tack stitch (point B to point C). If you are using silk ribbon, keep the tack stitch as flat as possible.

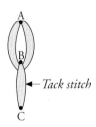

FEATHER STITCH

Use this stitch with silk ribbon as greenery, adding small buds in the Vs, or use it to outline the appliqués.

1. Bring the needle up at point A, down at point B, then up at point C.
2. Bring the needle down at point D and up at point E. Continue as shown.

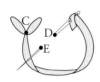

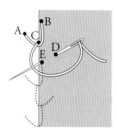

FERN

Use increasingly longer fly stitches (page 27) to create these lush ferns. Make sure the center stitches touch so the stem appears continuous.

1. Mark a guideline for the fern stem.
2. Make a straight stitch (page 33) at the top of the guideline, then make a fly stitch below the straight stitch on the guideline.
3. Continue adding fly stitches, gradually increasing the size of each stitch.

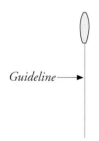

Guideline ⟶

FILLED BULLION-TIPPED FLOWER

1. Make a French knot (page 27) for the flower center.
2. Following instructions for a bullion-tipped flower (page 23), make 4 to 6 petals around the flower center.
3. Add a straight stitch (page 33) to the center of each bullion-tipped daisy stitch, using matching or contrasting embroidery floss, thread, or silk ribbon. If you are using silk ribbon, keep the ribbon flat.

FILLED LAZY DAISY

Combine a lazy daisy stitch with a straight stitch to make interesting leaves and petals. Use a second color of embroidery floss, thread, or silk ribbon to add interest.

1. Follow instructions for a lazy daisy stitch (page 29).
2. Add a straight stitch (page 33) inside the loop of the lazy daisy. Bring the needle up at point D and down at point E.

FILLED LAZY DAISY FLOWER

1. Make French knots (page 27) or stitch small beads for the flower center.
2. Following the instructions for a filled lazy daisy, make 4 to 6 petals around the flower center.

FISHBONE STITCH

This stitch is the basis for the fishbone stitch flower below.

1. Bring the needle up at point A, down at point B, then up at point C.
2. Bring the needle down at point D.
3. Repeat. Keep the distance between points B and C the same for each stitch; keep the distance between points A and D the same for each stitch.

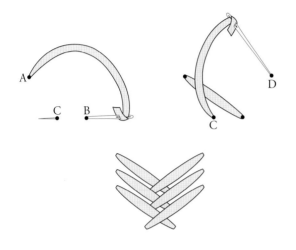

FISHBONE STITCH FLOWER

To make this flower, gradually increase the size of the fishbone stitch as you work downward.

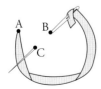

FLY STITCH

Use silk ribbon with this stitch to make small leaves that cradle a flower bud.

1. Bring the needle up at point A, down at point B, then up at point C.
2. Bring the needle down at point D.

FRENCH KNOT

Use this versatile stitch for flower centers or groups of tiny buds. If you are using silk ribbon, the flatter it is wrapped around the needle, the smaller the knot. If you want a puffy knot, keep your tension loose and allow your ribbon to twist as you wrap it around the needle.

1. Bring the needle up at point A.
2. Wrap the floss, thread, or ribbon around the tip of the needle 3 times.
3. Bring the needle down next to point A. Gently pull the floss, thread, or ribbon until a knot forms.

FRENCH KNOT FLOWER

Following the instructions above for a French knot, use yellow ribbon for the knot at the flower center, then surround it with different-colored knots for petals. Make 5 knots as shown.

GATHERED RIBBON STITCH

Use this stitch to make the upper part of the acorns in the Acorn Wreath block (page 53).

1. Thread one needle with a 12"-long piece of silk ribbon and a second needle with matching thread.
2. Bring both needles up at point A.
3. Using the second needle and a running stitch (page 32), stitch down the middle of the ribbon as shown.
4. Gently gather the ribbon to the desired length. To tack in place, bring the second needle to the back of the block and knot the thread.
5. To finish, bring the first needle to the back and knot the ribbon.

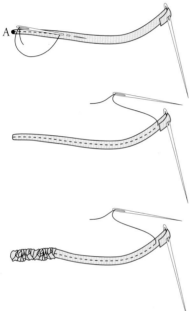

GATHERED RIBBON ROSE

In the traditional method for this stitch, you gather the length of ribbon, then tack the rose in place. I found this method awkward when I was working with 4mm silk ribbon, so I adapted the traditional stitch to gather and tack at the same time.

1. Thread one needle with a 12"-long piece of silk ribbon and a second needle with matching thread.
2. Bring both needles up at point A. This will be the center of the rose.
3. Using the second needle and a running stitch (page 32), stitch approximately 1" along one selvage edge of the ribbon.
4. Gently gather the ribbon. To tack in place, bring the second needle down at point B and up at point C.
5. Repeat steps 3 and 4, working in a spiral around point A, until the rose is the desired size.
6. Bring both needles to the back and knot the ribbon and thread.

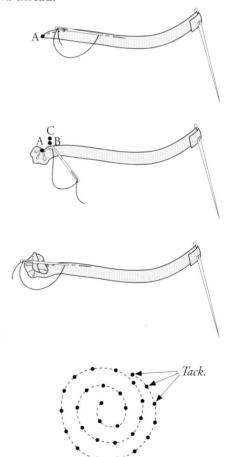

Tack.

HERRINGBONE STITCH

Use this woven stitch for the wing on the Roses with a Peacock block (page 76) and to make a herringbone stitch rose (below). If you are using silk ribbon, make sure to keep the ribbon flat as you stitch.

1. Bring the needle up at point A, down at point B, then up at point C.
2. Bring the needle down at point D and up at point E, halfway between points A and D.
3. Bring the needle down at point F and up at point G, halfway between points B and C.
4. Repeat steps 2 and 3, working from side to side. Always position the needle halfway between the previous stitch.

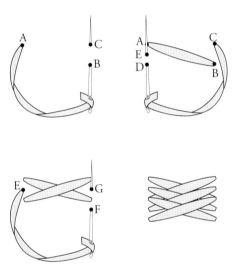

HERRINGBONE STITCH ROSE

This stitch looks like a side view of a rose, framed at the bottom with leaves. To add interest, twist a few of the petals.

1. Draw an oval the size of the desired rose on your background fabric.
2. Following the instructions above for a herringbone stitch, fill the oval with stitches.
3. To finish, make 2 ribbon stitches (page 30) on either side of the rose. These cover some of the rough stitch edges.

LAZY DAISY STITCH

This stitch works well as a leaf or as petals on a flower. Keep your loop as flat as possible.

1. Bring the needle up at point A, down at point B, then up at point C. Make sure the embroidery floss, thread, or silk ribbon is under the needle as shown.
2. Gently pull the floss, thread, or ribbon. Bring the needle down at point D (tack stitch).

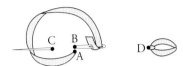

LAZY DAISY FLOWER

1. Make a French knot (page 27) or stitch a cluster of beads for the flower center.
2. Following the instructions for a lazy daisy stitch, make 4 to 6 petals around the flower center.

LOOP STITCH

This is just one method for making a loop stitch. This stitch works well for leaves and flower petals.

1. Bring the needle up at point A.
2. To create a loop, lay the ribbon on itself as shown. Bring the needle down through both layers of ribbon at point B.
3. Gently pull the ribbon through the layers until snug. If you pull the ribbon too tight, the loop will pull through the fabric. (I like to hold the loop on the front side with my thumb as I pull the ribbon through.)

LOOP STITCH DAISY

Use this full daisy in the Blooming Basket Block on page 60.

1. Make 5 to 8 French knots (page 27) for the flower center.
2. Following the instructions for a loop stitch, make 8 to 10 petals around the flower center. Space the petals evenly.
3. Make another row of loop stitches behind the first row, lifting the first row out of the way as you stitch.

LOOP STITCH FLOWER

This delightful flower is used in many of these miniature blocks.

1. Make 3 French knots (page 27) or stitch small beads for the flower center.
2. Following the instructions for the loop stitch, make 4 to 6 petals around the flower center.

MONTANO KNOTS

To create an impression of dimension in this cluster of knots, mix different colors of silk ribbon. Keep the ribbon loose on the needle and allow it to twist. Follow the instructions for a French knot (page 27), but wrap the ribbon around the needle 7 times for the large knots. Use fewer wraps to make smaller knots.

OPEN DAISY STITCH

Use this stitch to make the bottom of the acorns in the Acorn Wreath block (page 53).

1. Bring the needle up at point A, down at point B, then up at point C.
2. Bring the needle down at point D (tack stitch).

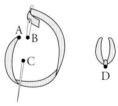

RIBBON STITCH

This is one of the most common silk-ribbon stitches. Use it to make leaves or flowers.

1. Bring the needle up at point A.
2. Lay the ribbon flat, then bring the needle down through the ribbon at point B.
3. Gently pull the ribbon through until the sides curl up to form the leaf-shaped stitch.

RIBBON STITCH DAISY

Be careful not to catch the ribbon on the back of your block; you could pull out the previous petals.

1. Make a French knot (page 27) or stitch a bead for the flower center.
2. Following the instructions for the ribbon stitch, make 8 petals around the flower center in the order shown.
3. To complete the daisy, add petals between each of the previous stitches.

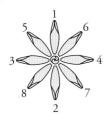 

RIBBON STITCH FLOWER

1. Make a French knot (page 27) or stitch a bead for the flower center.
2. Following the instructions for the ribbon stitch, make 6 petals around the flower center as shown.

ROUND BULLION ROSE

Try substituting whipstitches (page 35) for the bullion stitches in this rose.

1. Make French knots (page 27) or stitch beads for the flower center.
2. Following the instructions for the bullion stitch (page 22), make bullion stitches for the petals spiraling around the flower center.

RUCHED ROSE

These roses are lovely and always seem to attract a great deal of attention, but it takes patience and persistence to make them. Don't be surprised if it takes twenty minutes to gather the ribbon.

1. Cut a 12"-long piece of ribbon. Thread an appliqué needle with matching thread.
2. Using a running stitch (page 32), stitch back and forth across the width of the ribbon as shown. Make sure the thread goes over the edge of the ribbon at each turn.
3. As you stitch, gently pull the thread to gather the ribbon until snug. Do not let the gathers twist. Check to make sure you have a set of petals on either side of the gathers.
4. To tack the rose to the fabric, stitch one end of the ribbon in place for the flower center.
5. Spiral the gathered ribbon around the flower center, tacking the inside petals and leaving the outside petals free.
6. Continue the spiral, tacking the inside petals under the outside petals in the previous row until you have finished the length of ribbon. Tuck the ribbon end under the last row of petals; tack.
7. Tack any loose petals, then knot the thread on the back of the block.

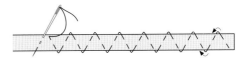

RUNNING (QUILTING) STITCH

1. Begin with a straight stitch (page 33). Bring the needle up at point A, the same distance away as the length of the straight stitch.
2. Bring the needle down at point B and up at point C. Make sure the stitches are even.

SATIN STITCH

Use this stitch to fill an area.

1. Begin with a straight stitch (page 33). Bring the needle up at point A and down at point B.
2. Continue stitching, placing the stitches side by side as shown and keeping them as neat as possible.

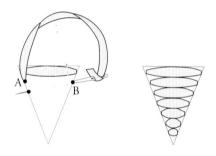

SCROLL STITCH ROSE

Keep your tension for this stitch loose.

1. Make 3 French knots (page 27) for flower center.
2. Bring the needle up at point A, down at point B, then up at point C.
3. Wrap the silk ribbon under the eye of the needle and under the tip as shown, then gently pull through.
4. Continue stitching in a spiral around the flower center. Repeat until the rose is the desired size.

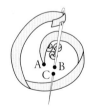

SPIDERWEB ROSE

This popular silk-ribbon rose is woven on a foundation stitch of five spokes and is simple to complete.

1. Thread one needle with a 12"-long piece of silk ribbon and a second needle with matching thread.
2. Bring the second needle up at point A, down at point B, then up at point C, keeping the stitches even.
3. Bring the needle down at point D.
4. Repeat steps 2 and 3, bringing the needle up at the center and over to one side. Repeat, bringing the needle over to the other side for the last spoke. Knot the thread on the back of the block.
5. Bring the needle with the silk ribbon up near the center of the web. Weave the ribbon over and under the spokes, without catching the spokes or the fabric. When the spokes are completely covered, knot the ribbon on the back of the block.

    If you have a slightly longer spoke that you can't cover with the ribbon, hide the end by adding a leaf. No one will ever know you made a mistake!

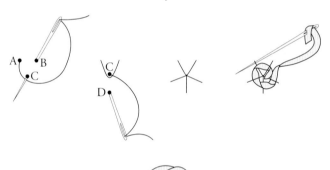

SPLIT STITCH

It is important for the ribbon to stay flat in this stitch.

1. Bring the needle up at point A, down at point B, then up at point C.
2. Bring the ribbon down at point D (through the ribbon) and up at point E.
3. Repeat, bringing the needle down through each previous stitch.

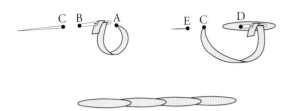

STEM STITCH

This stitch works well for outlining appliqués. Keep your thread on the side of the appliqué so the stitch will lie snugly against the edge of the fabric.

1. Make a small straight stitch (page 33). Bring the needle up at point A and down at point B, then up halfway between points A and B at point C.
2. Bring the needle down at point D and up at the end of the last stitch, point B.
3. Repeat, bringing the needle up at the end of each previous stitch.

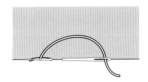

STEM STITCH ROSE

I have included two methods for a stem stitch rose. The second method makes a plumper rose.

Method 1

1. Make 3 French knots (page 27) or stitch beads for the flower center.
2. Work a stem stitch around the French knots, spiraling outward until it is the desired size.

Method 2

1. Work a stem stitch around the outside of the flower, spiraling inward to the center.
2. Make 3 French knots (page 27) or stitch beads for the flower center.

STRAIGHT STITCH

If you are using silk ribbon, keep the ribbon as flat as possible. Bring the needle up at A and down at B.

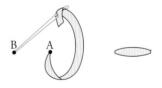

THREADED BACKSTITCH

Use this stitch for the vertical weave in the Blooming Basket block (page 60).

1. Using one color of embroidery floss, make a backstitch (page 22).
2. Using a contrasting color of floss, weave in and out of the backstitch.
3. Using the floss from step 2, weave in the opposite direction to create a chainlike stitch.

TWISTED CHAIN STITCH

This stitch is perfect for making silk-ribbon rosebuds. Use these buds with feather-stitch greenery.

1. Bring the needle up at point A and down at point B, then bring the tip of the needle up at point C, but do not pull the needle through.
2. Wrap silk ribbon over and under the tip of the needle as shown.
3. Pull the ribbon through at point C and down at point D.

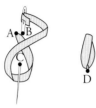

TWISTED RIBBON FLOWER

I discovered this flower while learning to make a twisted ribbon rose. I liked the cone-shaped flower that formed as I pulled the ribbon.

1. Follow the instructions for a twisted ribbon rose.
2. Gently pull the needle and ribbon through the fabric until a twisted cone forms.
3. Push the twisted cone on its side, against the fabric, and tack with matching thread.
4. Frame the flower with ribbon stitch leaves (page 30).

TWISTED RIBBON ROSE

This rose turns out different every time you make it. If the rose doesn't turn out the way you want, take out the stitch and iron the ribbon. For a larger rose, add a row of stem stitches (page 33) around the rose.

1. Thread one needle with a 12"-long piece of silk ribbon and a second needle with matching thread.
2. Bring the needle and ribbon up in the center of the rose (point A). Twist the ribbon until tight. (Stop before the ribbon begins to kink.)
3. Pinch the ribbon halfway down the twisted length and fold it in half.
4. Allow the two halves to twist together. Bring the needle back down at point B.
5. Gently pull the needle through the fabric, letting the twists form the rose.
6. Tack the rose to the block, using matching thread.

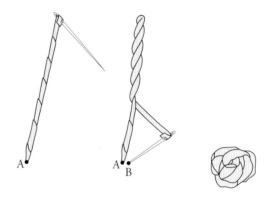

WHIPSTITCH

Vary the size of this bud by changing the length of the straight stitch or the number of wraps.

1. Make a straight stitch (page 33) the length of the desired bud.
2. Push the straight stitch aside and bring the needle up underneath the stitch.
3. Wrap the embroidery floss, thread, or silk ribbon around the straight stitch. If you are using silk ribbon, keep the ribbon as flat as possible.
4. To finish, push the stitch aside and bring the needle to the back of the block.

WHIPPED SPIDERWEB ROSE

This rose turns out more star shaped than round.

1. Follow the instructions for a spiderweb rose, steps 1–4, to make the web (page 32).
2. Bring the needle and silk ribbon up near the center of the web.
3. Wrap the ribbon around each spoke, working outward until the spokes are completely covered.
4. Bring the ribbon to the back of the block and knot.

WOUND RIBBON ROSE

1. Thread one needle with a 12"-long piece of silk ribbon and a second needle with matching thread.
2. Place a pin as shown, taking an ⅛"-long "bite" out of the block. This will be the center of the flower.
3. Bring the needle and silk ribbon up at point C, next to the pin. Wrap the ribbon around the pin 7 or 8 times, twisting the ribbon slightly as you wrap.
4. Bring the ribbon to the back of the block and knot.
5. Bring the second needle with thread up under the twists. Tack the ribbon at even intervals.
6. Remove the pin.
7. Make French knots (page 27) or stitch beads in the center if desired.

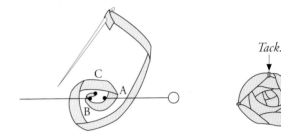

Tack.

ADDING BEADS

There are many ways to attach beads to quilt blocks. This is my favorite method.

1. Bring the needle up through the fabric, through the bead, then back down through the fabric. Repeat, stitching through the bead twice.
2. Slide the next bead onto the needle and repeat step 1.
3. Run the needle and thread back through the length of the beads to straighten them. Knot the thread on the back of the block.

BEADING THREAD
When choosing thread, pick a color that matches the background fabric rather than the beads. The thread will blend into the background fabric.

GALLERY OF BLOCKS

Acorn Wreath (page 53)

Album Wreath (page 54)

Baltimore Mansion (page 55)

Beaded Basket (page 56)

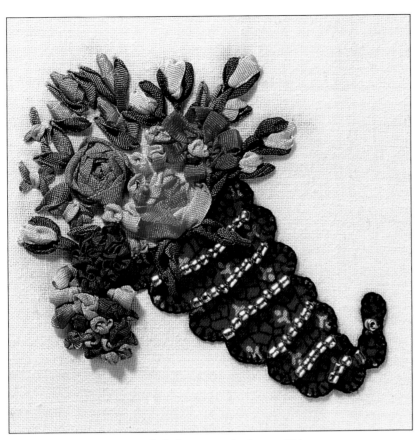

Beaded Cornucopia (page 58)

Beribboned Bouquet (page 59)

Blooming Basket (page 60)

Bountiful Cornucopia (page 62)

Bouquet of Roses (page 63)

Cactus Reel (page 64)

Cherry Wreath (page 65)

Clipper Ship (page 66)

Country Cabin (page 67)

Eagle (page 68)

Feathered Heart (page 69)

Grapevine Wreath (page 70)

Heart Wreath (page 71)

Library (page 72)

Lyre (page 73)

Oak Reel (page 74)

Open Wreath (page 75)

Roses with a Peacock (page 76)

Rose Wreath (page 77)

Strawberry Wreath (page 78)

Traditional Red Basket (page 79)

Urn with Roses (page 81)

Vase of Flowers (page 82)

Woven Basket (page 83)

Grapevine Border (page 92)

Rose Garland Border (page 93)

Swag Border (page 94)

BLOCK PATTERNS

For detailed instructions on constructing and embroidering these blocks, refer to "Constructing the Blocks" on pages 10–12 and "Embroidering the Blocks" on pages 21–35. Do not worry about following these patterns exactly. Use the illustrations and photographs as guides for flower placement and ideas. After outlining the appliqué pieces, place the block over the pattern for a general idea of flower arrangement. Since everyone's stitch tension is slightly different, your flowers may not turn out exactly the same size as mine. If you have any obvious open spaces, fill in with small flowers, buds, leaves, or French knots.

CHARMING BLOCKS

You may want to add small brass charms to liven up your blocks. For example, leaf and butterfly charms are a wonderful way to embellish a basket or vase. This is an opportunity to display your personality and sense of humor.

Acorn Wreath

COLOR PHOTO ON PAGE 37

With all the floral designs in this collection, it is nice to have a quilt block with an unusual motif. Use two colors of silk ribbon to make the acorns look more realistic.

1. Trace, cut, and fuse the leaves and bows.
2. Using a stem stitch, outline the leaves, stems, and bow with embroidery floss or thread.
3. The acorns in this block are a combination of two different stitches with silk ribbon: an open daisy and gathered ribbon. Make the open daisy stitch first, then add 2 rows of gathered ribbon stitches for the top of the acorn.

Appliqué Pieces

Stitches

 Gathered ribbon stitch (page 28)

Open daisy stitch (page 30)

Outline Stitch

—·—· Stem stitch (page 33)

Placement and Embroidery Guide

Album Wreath

COLOR PHOTO ON PAGE 37

Album blocks are often the central focus in antique Baltimore Album quilts. They are usually surrounded by birds and wreaths, or set in baskets of flowers. The album is often red and may be signed "Album" or "Bible." If desired, use a .005 Pigma pen to sign your book. (See "Signing Your Blocks" on page 11.)

1. Trace, cut, and fuse the bird, wings, book, and bow.
2. Using a stem stitch, outline the main stem of the wreath and the small flower stems with embroidery floss or thread.
3. Using a chain stitch, outline the bow.
4. Using a stem stitch, outline the bird.
5. Using a French knot, make the bird's eye.
6. Using a satin stitch, fill in the bird's beak.
7. Using a stem stitch, outline the book and binding.
8. Fill in the wreath with silk-ribbon stitches as shown.

Appliqué Pieces

Stitches

 Bullion-tipped daisy (page 23)

 Cross-stitch flower (page 25)

 Fishbone stitch flower (page 27)

 French knot (page 27)

 Lazy daisy stitch (page 29)

 Ribbon stitch (page 30)

 Twisted ribbon rose (page 34)

 Whipped spiderweb rose (page 35)

Outline Stitches

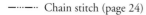
Chain stitch (page 24)
Satin stitch (page 32)
Stem stitch (page 33)

Placement and Embroidery Guide

BALTIMORE MANSION
COLOR PHOTO ON PAGE 38

Houses are some of the more unusual motifs in antique Baltimore Album quilts. This one is modeled after the Georgian-style houses found in these quilts.

1. Trace, cut, and fuse the house, roof, chimneys, windows, window trims, door, door trim, grass, sidewalks, and tree.

2. Using a buttonhole stitch, outline the house, roof, chimneys, door, and outer sidewalk with embroidery floss or thread.

3. Using a backstitch, outline the windows, window trims, and door trim.

4. Using a stem stitch, outline the tree, door center, and inner sidewalk.

5. Using a feather stitch, outline the grass.

6. Using a straight stitch, stitch the fence posts and windowpanes. Couch the crossbars on the fence posts.

7. Referring to "Adding Beads" on page 36, attach beads for the pillars and doorknobs.

8. Fill in with silk-ribbon stitches as shown.

Appliqué Pieces

Stitches

○ French knot (page 27)

▢ Loop stitch (page 29)

⬭ Ribbon stitch (page 30)

Outline Stitches

- - - - - Backstitch (page 22)
– – Buttonhole stitch (page 23)
⌁ Feather stitch (page 26)
–·–·– Stem stitch (page 33)
—— Straight stitch (page 33)

Placement and Embroidery Guide

BEADED BASKET

COLOR PHOTO ON PAGE 38

Embellish this basket with rows of beads and a narrow, picot-edged rayon braid. Coordinate the basket fabric, beads, and braid colors.

1. Trace, cut, and fuse the basket, base, and diamond-shaped accents. Use different fabrics for the base pieces.

2. Using a satin stitch, attach pieces of rayon braid as shown. Stitch the ends of each piece; with matching thread, make tiny running stitches down the center.

3. Referring to "Adding Beads" on page 36, stitch beads across the basket rim, center, and base as shown. Stitch the beads snugly against each other. Make sure to completely cover the raw edges of the braid at the basket rim.

4. Using a stem stitch, outline pieces #1 and #2 (basket base) and the diamond-shaped accents with embroidery floss or thread.

5. Fill the basket with silk-ribbon stitches as shown. Stitch the ferns before the flowers.

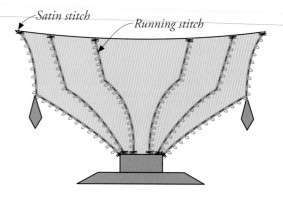

Satin stitch *Running stitch*

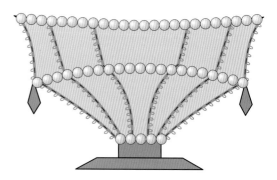

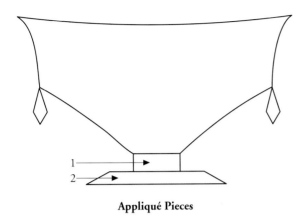

Appliqué Pieces

Placement and Embroidery Guide

Stitches

Bullion-tipped daisy (page 23)

Fern (page 26)

Lazy daisy stitch (page 29)

Loop stitch daisy (page 30)

Ribbon stitch (page 30)

Ribbon stitch daisy (page 31)

Twisted chain stitch (page 34)

Wound ribbon rose (page 35)

Outline Stitch

Stem stitch (page 33)

BEADED CORNUCOPIA

COLOR PHOTO ON PAGE 39

Use beads to define the segments in this cornucopia. Coordinate the beads with the fabric or, for a more traditional look, use red or blue fabric with yellow or gold beads.

1. Trace, cut, and fuse the cornucopia.
2. Using a buttonhole stitch, outline the cornucopia with embroidery floss or thread.
3. Referring to "Adding Beads" on page 36, stitch beads across the cornucopia segments.
4. Fill in with silk-ribbon stitches as shown.

Appliqué Piece

Placement and Embroidery Guide

Stitches

⟋	Bullion-tipped daisy (page 23)
✕	Cross-stitch flower (page 25)
⋎	Feather stitch (page 26)
○	French knot (page 27)
Ⓕ	Gathered ribbon rose (page 28)
Ⓒ	Herringbone stitch rose (page 29)
⟋	Lazy daisy stitch (page 29)
Ⓗ	Loop stitch flower (page 30)
⟋	Ribbon stitch (page 30)
Ⓔ	Spiderweb rose (page 32)
⟑	Twisted chain stitch (page 34)
⟮	Whipstitch (page 35)

Outline Stitch

– – Buttonhole stitch (page 23)

BERIBBONED BOUQUET

COLOR PHOTO ON PAGE 39

Bouquets are a common motif in antique Baltimore Album quilts, especially with the triple-knot bow as in this block. To add interest, make a silk-ribbon bow instead of the fabric bow.

1. Trace, cut, and fuse the bow.
2. Using a stem stitch, outline the bow with embroidery floss or thread.
3. Fill the basket with silk-ribbon stitches as shown. Stitch the ferns before the flowers.

Appliqué Piece

Placement and Embroidery Guide

Stitches

Bullion-tipped daisy (page 23)
Couched ribbon stem (page 25)
Cross-stitch flower (page 25)
Feather stitch (page 26)
Fern (page 26)
French knot (page 27)
Gathered ribbon rose (page 28)
Lazy daisy stitch (page 29)
Lazy daisy flower (page 29)
Loop stitch flower (page 30)
Ribbon stitch (page 30)
Scroll stitch rose (page 32)
Spiderweb rose (page 32)
Stem stitch (page 33)
Twisted chain stitch (page 34)
Whipstitch (page 35)

Outline Stitch

—·— Stem stitch (page 33)

BLOOMING BASKET

COLOR PHOTO ON PAGE 40

Gimp and embroidery give this block a slightly heavier look. Choose a subtle print for the appliqué to prevent it from overpowering the other blocks.

1. Trace, cut, and fuse the basket, base, and bow.
2. Using a stem stitch, outline pieces #1 and #2 of the base and the bow with embroidery floss or thread.
3. Using a threaded backstitch, stitch the basket handle and vertical spokes. Use more than 2 strands of floss so the handle and spokes are the same width as the halved gimp (see step 4).
4. Cut the gimp in half through the center as shown. Use half of the gimp to trim the basket.
5. Using a satin stitch, attach a piece of gimp to one end of the basket rim. Couch the gimp along the top of the basket, then use a satin stitch to attach the other end. Repeat for the bottom of the basket.
6. Fill the basket with silk-ribbon stitches as shown.

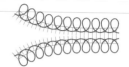

Cut in half through the center.

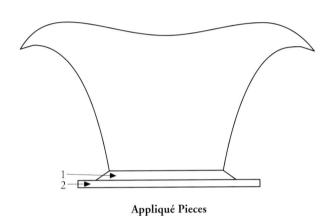

Appliqué Pieces

Placement and Embroidery Guide

Stitches

Bullion-tipped daisy (page 23)

V Buttonhole stitch flower (page 23)

Elongated lazy daisy (page 25)

Feather stitch (page 26)

○ French knot (page 27)

F Gathered ribbon rose (page 28)

Lazy daisy stitch (page 29)

Ribbon stitch (page 30)

U Ribbon stitch daisy (page 31)

W Stem stitch rose (page 33)

Whipstitch (page 35)

Outline Stitches

—·—· Stem stitch (page 33)

··········· Threaded backstitch (page 33)

BOUNTIFUL CORNUCOPIA
COLOR PHOTO ON PAGE 40

You have two options for the cornucopia: use one fabric and embroider the segments in a complementary color, or use two or more fabrics to make the segments. If you use two or more fabrics, cut and fuse the cornucopia in one fabric, then fuse different-colored segments on top.

1. Trace, cut, and fuse the cornucopia.
2. Using a stem stitch, outline the cornucopia segments with embroidery floss or thread.
3. Fill in with silk-ribbon stitches as shown.

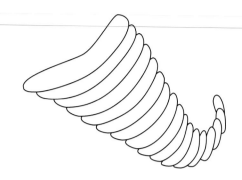

Appliqué Pieces

Placement and Embroidery Guide

Stitches

Bullion-tipped daisy (page 23)
D — Chain stitch rose (page 24)
✕ — Cross-stitch flower (page 25)
⋎ — Feather stitch (page 26)
○ — French knot (page 27)
F — Gathered ribbon rose (page 28)
Lazy daisy stitch (page 29)
I — Lazy daisy flower (page 29)
Ribbon stitch (page 30)
K — Ribbon stitch flower (page 31)
E — Spiderweb rose (page 32)
Twisted chain stitch (page 34)
Whipstitch (page 35)

Outline Stitch

—·— Stem stitch (page 33)

BOUQUET OF ROSES
COLOR PHOTO ON PAGE 41

This is one of my favorite blocks. To make fuller blooms, try Method 2 for the stem stitch rose.

1. Trace, cut, and fuse the bow.
2. Using a stem stitch, outline the bow with embroidery floss or thread.
3. Fill with silk-ribbon stitches as shown. Stitch the ferns before the flowers.

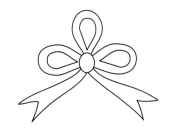

Appliqué Piece

Placement and Embroidery Guide

Stitches

Bullion-tipped daisy (page 23)

French knot (page 27)

Lazy daisy stitch (page 29)

Ribbon stitch (page 30)

Stem stitch (page 33)

Stem stitch rose (page 33)

Outline Stitch

—·— Stem stitch (page 33)

CACTUS REEL
COLOR PHOTO ON PAGE 41

Antique Baltimore Album quilts often include red-and-green folk-art blocks, such as this Cactus Reel. These simple blocks contrast well with the ornate floral blocks.

1. Trace, cut, and fuse the leaves.
2. Using a buttonhole stitch, outline the small leaves with embroidery floss or thread.
3. Using a stem stitch, outline the large leaves.
4. Fill in with silk-ribbon stitches as shown.

Appliqué Pieces

Stitches

 Coral stitch rose (page 24)

 Couched ribbon stem (page 25)

Lazy daisy stitch (page 29)

Outline Stitches

– – Buttonhole stitch (page 23)

–·–·– Stem stitch (page 33)

Placement and Embroidery Guide

CHERRY WREATH

COLOR PHOTO ON PAGE 42

This block is easy and quick, which makes it especially good for a beginner. Like the Cactus Reel, this block is traditionally red and green.

1. Trace, cut, and fuse the leaves.
2. Using a stem stitch, outline the leaves with embroidery floss or thread, then add the stems.
3. Fill in with silk-ribbon stitches as shown.

Stitch

○   French knot (page 27)

Outline Stitch

—·—·—   Stem stitch (page 33)

Appliqué Pieces

Placement and Embroidery Guide

CLIPPER SHIP
COLOR PHOTO ON PAGE 42

This is one of my most popular Miniature Baltimore Album blocks. Make sure there is enough contrast between the background and sail fabrics, as well as between the background fabric and the thread you use for the rigging.

1. Trace, cut, and fuse the ship body (two pieces), sails, flags, and water.
2. Using a stem stitch, outline the ship body, sails, and flags with embroidery floss or thread.
3. Using a chain stitch, outline the water.
4. Use a stem stitch for the masts.
5. Using a straight stitch, stitch the rigging.
6. Embellish the flags as shown with a .005 Pigma pen.
7. Fill in with silk-ribbon stitches as shown.

Appliqué Pieces

Stitches

(D) Chain stitch rose (page 24)

Elongated lazy daisy (page 25)

Feather stitch (page 26)

○ French knot (page 27)

(F) Gathered ribbon rose (page 28)

Lazy daisy stitch (page 29)

Ribbon stitch (page 30)

Outline Stitches

----- Chain stitch (page 24)

—·— Stem stitch (page 33)

——— Straight stitch (page 33)

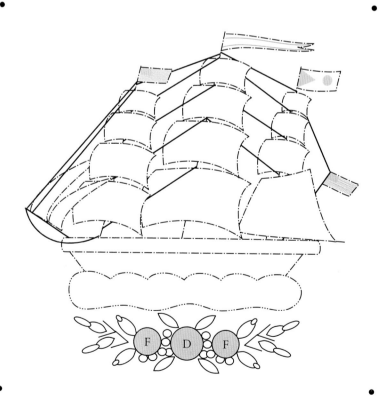

Placement and Embroidery Guide

COUNTRY CABIN
COLOR PHOTO ON PAGE 43

There were very few antique Baltimore Album quilts with Country Cabin blocks, but that didn't stop me from including it. This is a favorite block for my students to embellish. See if you can come up with some innovative ways to make this cabin unique.

1. Trace, cut, and fuse the house, roof, chimneys, windows, door, grass, sidewalk, and tree.
2. Using a stem stitch, outline the house, door, windows, and tree with embroidery floss or thread.
3. Using a buttonhole stitch, outline the sidewalk, roof, and chimneys.
4. Using a chain stitch, outline the grass.
5. Using a straight stitch, stitch the shutters and door.
6. Fill in with silk-ribbon stitches as shown.

Appliqué Pieces

Stitches

○ French knot (page 27)

▯ Loop stitch (page 29)

◗ Ribbon stitch (page 30)

♢ Twisted chain stitch (page 34)

Outline Stitches

– – Buttonhole stitch (page 23)

····· Chain stitch (page 24)

–·–· Stem stitch (page 33)

——— Straight stitch (page 33)

Placement and Embroidery Guide

EAGLE
COLOR PHOTO ON PAGE 43

Patriotism—represented by an American eagle—is a common theme in antique Baltimore Album quilts. To make the flag extra special, use variegated white-and-blue ribbon for the field of stars.

1. Trace, cut, and fuse the stars and shield, and eagle body, wings, and head.
2. Using a stem stitch, outline the stars and shield, and eagle body, wings, and head with embroidery floss or thread. Stitch the arrow shafts.
3. Using a satin stitch, stitch the arrowheads and the eagle beak and claw.
4. Using a chain stitch, stitch the flagpole.
5. Using a straight stitch, fill the shield as shown.
6. Using a split stitch, stitch the stripes on the flag.
7. To make the tassels on the flagpole, stitch 4 straight stitches, wrap them with a contrasting color of thread, and gather.
8. Fill in with silk-ribbon stitches as shown. Use a stem stitch for the flower stems.

Appliqué Pieces

Stitches

○ French knot (page 27)

◗ Ribbon stitch (page 30)

Ⓜ Ruched rose (page 31)

✗ Twisted chain stitch (page 34)

◖ Whipstitch (page 35)

Outline Stitches

--•--- Chain stitch (page 24)

⸳⸳⸳⸳⸳⸳ Satin stitch (page 32)

═══ Split stitch (page 33)

--•-- Stem stitch (page 33)

──── Straight stitch (page 33)

Placement and Embroidery Guide

FEATHERED HEART

COLOR PHOTO ON PAGE 44

To create an illusion of reverse appliqué, embroider the feathers in the same color as the background fabric.

1. Trace, cut, and fuse the feather heart.
2. Using a stem stitch, outline the feathers with embroidery floss or thread.
3. Fill in with silk-ribbon stitches as shown. Use a stem stitch for the flower stems.

MARKING THE STITCHING LINES

Mark the design on the paper side of fusible web with a black permanent marker, then fuse the web to the wrong side of your appliqué fabric. Do not remove the paper backing. Using a light table or window, trace the stitching lines on the appliqué before you cut and fuse it to the block.

Stitches

 Filled lazy daisy (page 26)

 Spiderweb rose (page 32)

Outline Stitch

—·—·— Stem stitch (page 33)

Appliqué Piece

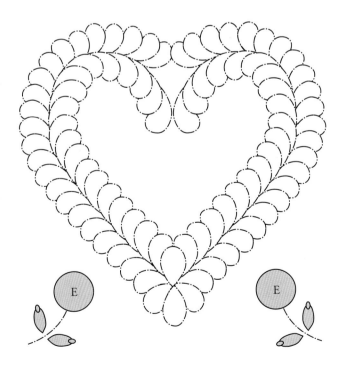

Placement and Embroidery Guide

Grapevine Wreath
COLOR PHOTO ON PAGE 44

Vary the sizes of the knots and use different colors of silk ribbon to make realistic grape clusters.

1. Trace, cut, and fuse the leaves.
2. Using a buttonhole stitch, outline the leaves with embroidery floss or thread.
3. Fill in with silk-ribbon stitches as shown. Using a stem stitch, make the grapevine.

Appliqué Pieces

Stitch

 Montano knots (page 30)

Outline Stitches

– – Buttonhole stitch (page 23)
–·–·– Stem stitch (page 33)

Placement and Embroidery Guide

Heart Wreath

COLOR PHOTO ON PAGE 45

Roses are the focal point of this traditional block. Make all the roses the same color or, for a little fun, balance two to four colors of roses around the wreath.

1. Trace, cut, and fuse the bow and leaves.
2. Using a chain stitch, outline the bow and leaves with embroidery floss or thread.
3. Fill in with silk-ribbon stitches as shown. Using a stem stitch, make the heart.

Appliqué Pieces

Stitch

 Gathered ribbon rose (page 28)

Outline Stitches

————·· Chain stitch (page 24)
—·—·— Stem stitch (page 33)

Placement and Embroidery Guide

LIBRARY
COLOR PHOTO ON PAGE 45

Landmark buildings and monuments did not escape the original designers of Baltimore Album quilts. I redesigned this building in miniature as a library. The weeping willow trees were an afterthought. There are many examples in antique Victorian needlework that include these trees.

1. Trace, cut, and fuse the building, dome, windows, shutters, trim, door, transom, foundation, steps, ground, and trees.

2. Using a chain stitch, outline the building and foundation with embroidery floss or thread.

3. Using a stem stitch, outline the dome, windows, shutters, door, trim, and trees.

4. Using a backstitch, outline the steps.

5. Using a buttonhole stitch, outline the ground.

6. Using a straight stitch, stitch the windowpanes.

7. Fill in with silk-ribbon stitches as shown. Using a fly stitch, stitch the weeping willow branches.

8. Stitch a bead for the doorknob.

Appliqué Pieces

Stitch

○ French knot (page 27)

Outline Stitches

- - - - Backstitch (page 22)
– – Buttonhole stitch (page 23)
–·–·– Chain stitch (page 24)
●●● Fly stitch (page 27)
–·–·– Stem stitch (page 33)
───── Straight stitch (page 33)

Placement and Embroidery Guide

LYRE
COLOR PHOTO ON PAGE 46

This block represents a musical theme. Mark the wreath stem line on your block so you don't exceed the finished block size. Try using a metallic thread for the lyre strings.

1. Trace, cut, and fuse the bow and lyre.
2. Using a stem stitch, outline the lyre with embroidery floss or thread.
3. Using a chain stitch, outline the bow.
4. Using a stem stitch, stitch the lyre strings and wreath stem.
5. Fill in with silk-ribbon stitches as shown.

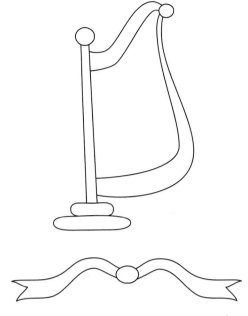

Appliqué Pieces

Stitches

- G Bullion-tipped flower (page 23)
- D Chain stitch rose (page 24)
- ✕ Cross-stitch flower (page 25)
- ⋎ Feather stitch (page 26)
- L French knot flower (page 27)
- Lazy daisy stitch (page 29)
- Loop stitch (page 29)
- Ribbon stitch (page 30)
- E Spiderweb rose (page 32)
- Twisted chain stitch (page 34)

Outline Stitches

—·—· Chain stitch (page 24)
—·—· Stem stitch (page 33)

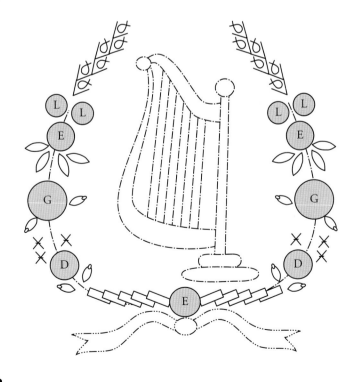

Placement and Embroidery Guide

OAK REEL
COLOR PHOTO ON PAGE 46

This is another popular red-and-green folk-art block. If you want to use red and green for this block, make sure those colors don't overpower or compete with the colors in your other quilt blocks.

1. Cut piece #1 as a circle and fuse. Cut and fuse the #2 pieces onto piece #1. Fuse the leaves.
2. Using a stem stitch, outline the reel with embroidery floss or thread.
3. Using a chain stitch, outline the leaves.
4. Fill in with silk-ribbon stitches as shown.

Appliqué Pieces

Stitches

Y   Fly stitch (page 27)

   Ribbon stitch (page 30)

   Twisted chain stitch (page 34)

Outline Stitches

········ Chain stitch (page 24)

─·─·─ Stem stitch (page 33)

Placement and Embroidery Guide

OPEN WREATH
COLOR PHOTO ON PAGE 47

This block is one of the best for calligraphy; it can look rather plain unless the center includes something special.

1. Trace, cut, and fuse the base.
2. Using a stem stitch, outline the base with embroidery floss or thread.
3. Fill in with silk-ribbon stitches as shown. Using a split stitch, make the wreath stem.

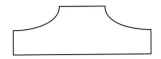

Appliqué Piece

Stitches

 Ribbon stitch (page 30)

 Twisted ribbon rose (page 34)

Outline Stitches

═══ Split stitch (page 33)

—·—· Stem stitch (page 33)

Placement and Embroidery Guide

ROSES WITH A PEACOCK

COLOR PHOTO ON PAGE 47

Birds—especially peacocks—are a special feature of antique Baltimore Album quilts. The herringbone stitch for the bird wing is optional; this is also the perfect spot to showcase a wonderful print.

1. Trace, cut, and fuse the branches, leaves, bird, and wing. Tuck some of the leaves under the branches before fusing.
2. Using a stem stitch, outline the branches, bird, and wing with embroidery floss or thread.
3. Using a chain stitch, outline the leaves.
4. Using a satin stitch, fill in the bird beak.
5. Fill in with silk-ribbon stitches as shown. Use a herringbone stitch for the bird wing if desired.

Appliqué Pieces

Stitches

○   French knot (page 27)

    Lazy daisy stitch (page 29)

Ⓔ   Spiderweb rose (page 32)

Outline Stitches

------ Chain stitch (page 24)

||||||||| Satin stitch (page 32)

-·-·- Stem stitch (page 33)

Placement and Embroidery Guide

ROSE WREATH
COLOR PHOTO ON PAGE 48

People have called me crazy for ruching the 4mm ribbon for these roses, but they love the finished block. With a little patience, you can create a beautiful block.

1. Trace, cut, and fuse the leaves.
2. Using a stem stitch, outline the leaves and stitch the wreath stem with embroidery floss or thread.
3. Fill in with silk-ribbon stitches as shown.

Appliqué Pieces

Stitches

 Ribbon stitch (page 30)

(M) Ruched rose (page 31)

 Twisted chain stitch (page 34)

Outline Stitch

—·—·— Stem stitch (page 33)

Placement and Embroidery Guide

Strawberry Wreath

COLOR PHOTO ON PAGE 48

Use ribbon to make fruit instead of flowers. Be careful when you make the dots on the strawberries with the Pigma pen; practice first, because it may bleed and needs a light touch.

1. Trace, cut, and fuse the leaves.
2. Using a stem stitch, outline the leaves and stitch the wreath stem with embroidery floss or thread.
3. Fill in with silk-ribbon stitches as shown. To make the strawberries, combine filled lazy daisy and ribbon stitches. Make the filled lazy daisy with red ribbon, then make 3 ribbon stitches with green ribbon.

 Make ribbon stitch on top of the filled lazy daisy stitch.

4. Make dots on the strawberries with a .005 Pigma pen after blocking the quilt block, so the ink does not disappear when you wet the block.

Stitches

 Filled lazy daisy (page 26)

 Ribbon stitch (page 30)

Outline Stitch

–·–·– Stem stitch (page 33)

Appliqué Pieces

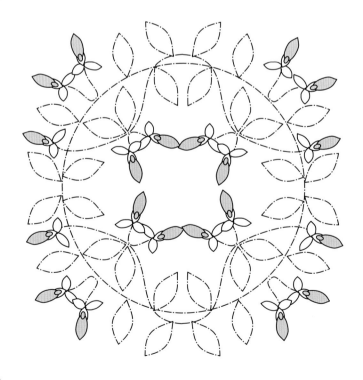

Placement and Embroidery Guide

TRADITIONAL RED BASKET
COLOR PHOTO ON PAGE 49

This is the signature-style basket commonly identified with antique Baltimore Album quilts. The baskets often included a prominent white rose. Let the leaves spray down over the braid of the basket for a more natural look.

1. Trace, cut, and fuse the pieces for the basket base. Use a different fabric for pieces #1 and #3 than for piece #2.

2. To make a woven basket, use a satin stitch to attach pieces of ⅛"-wide rayon braid for the body of the basket as shown. Use tacky glue or clear fingernail polish on the ends to prevent fraying. Satin-stitch the ends of each piece; then with matching thread, make tiny running stitches down the center. Cover the ends of the braid with pieces for the handle, rim, and base. Tuck the curved end underneath the other braid at point A.

3. Using a stem stitch, outline pieces #1 and #2 of the basket base with embroidery floss or thread.

4. Using a buttonhole stitch, outline piece #3.

5. Fill the basket with silk-ribbon stitches as shown.

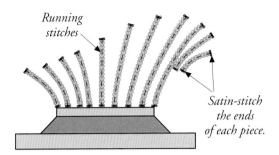

Running stitches

Satin-stitch the ends of each piece.

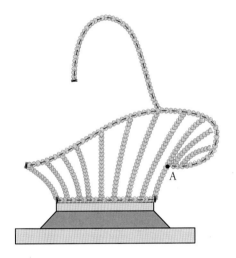

A

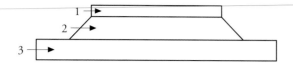

Appliqué Pieces

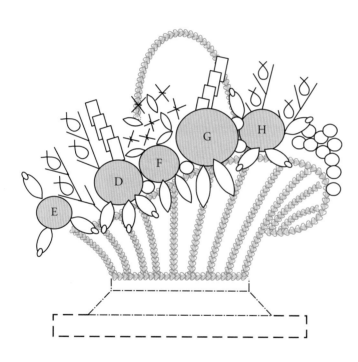

Placement and Embroidery Guide

Stitches

Ⓖ Bullion-tipped flower (page 23)

Ⓓ Chain stitch rose (page 24)

✕ Cross-stitch flower (page 25)

Ⓨ Feather stitch (page 26)

◯ French knot (page 27)

Ⓕ Gathered ribbon rose (page 28)

◊ Lazy daisy stitch (page 29)

▭ Loop stitch (page 29)

Ⓗ Loop stitch flower (page 30)

◊ Ribbon stitch (page 30)

Ⓔ Spiderweb rose (page 32)

◊ Twisted chain stitch (page 34)

Outline Stitches

– – Buttonhole stitch (page 23)

–·–·– Stem stitch (page 33)

Urn with Roses

COLOR PHOTO ON PAGE 49

Fill this urn to overflowing. Your fabric choices can make this block extra special.

1. Trace, cut, and fuse the urn, tear-shaped decorations, and base pieces #1 and #2. Mark the tear-shaped decorations on the paper-backed fusible web when marking the urn, then cut the decorations from the urn fabric before you cut out the urn. Fuse a piece of fabric for the decorations on the background fabric, then fuse the urn on top.
2. Using a stem stitch, outline the urn with embroidery floss or thread.
3. Using a satin stitch, fill in the urn stand.
4. Referring to "Adding Beads" on page 36, stitch beads on the urn handles and across the urn center.
5. Fill in with silk-ribbon stitches as shown.

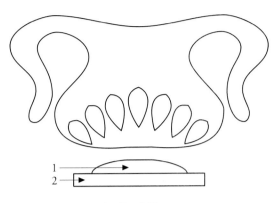

Appliqué Pieces

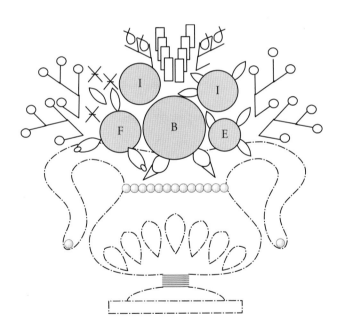

Placement and Embroidery Guide

Stitches

(B) Bullion rose (page 23)

Bullion-tipped daisy (page 23)

✕ Cross-stitch flower (page 25)

Y Feather stitch (page 26)

○ French knot (page 27)

(F) Gathered ribbon rose (page 28)

Lazy daisy stitch (page 29)

(I) Lazy daisy flower (page 29)

▯ Loop stitch (page 29)

Ribbon stitch (page 30)

(E) Spiderweb rose (page 32)

Twisted chain stitch (page 34)

Outline Stitches

▨▨▨ Satin stitch (page 32)

—·—·— Stem stitch (page 33)

Vase of Flowers
COLOR PHOTO ON PAGE 50

Be careful not to extend beyond the finished size of this block.

1. Trace, cut, and fuse the vase, decorations, and base. Mark the decorations on the paper-backed fusible web when marking the vase, then cut the decorations from the vase fabric before you cut out the vase. Fuse a piece of fabric for the decorations on the background fabric, then fuse the vase on top.
2. Using a stem stitch, outline the vase and its base with embroidery floss or thread.
3. Stitch beads on the vase handles and at the bottom of the vase.
4. Fill in with silk-ribbon stitches as shown. Use a stem stitch for the flower stems.

Appliqué Pieces

Placement and Embroidery Guide

Stitches

🖊	Bullion-tipped daisy (page 23)
T	Filled bullion-tipped flower (page 26)
O	French knot (page 27)
L	French knot flower (page 27)
F	Gathered ribbon rose (page 28)
◗	Lazy daisy stitch (page 29)
H	Loop stitch flower (page 30)
◖	Ribbon stitch (page 30)
R	Round bullion rose (page 31)
✕	Twisted chain stitch (page 34)
S	Twisted ribbon flower (page 34)

Outline Stitch

—·—·— Stem stitch (page 33)

Woven Basket

COLOR PHOTO ON PAGE 50

Create an incredibly realistic basket using Bunka braid. To prevent the background fabric from puckering, place this block in a hoop as you weave.

1. Trace, cut, and fuse the basket rim, base, and diamond-shaped accents.

2. Using matching thread, couch pieces #1 and #2 of braid for the basket sides as shown.

3. Couch pieces #3 and #4 as shown. Do not couch the bottom half of the braid. Repeat for pieces #5 and #6. Begin weaving the pieces over and under at the bottom of the basket. Continue adding pieces and weaving.

4. To finish the basket, couch a piece of braid in a curve as shown.

5. Using a stem stitch, outline the rim, base, and accents with embroidery floss or thread.

6. Using a chain stitch, make the handles on the basket sides.

7. Fill the basket with silk-ribbon stitches as shown.

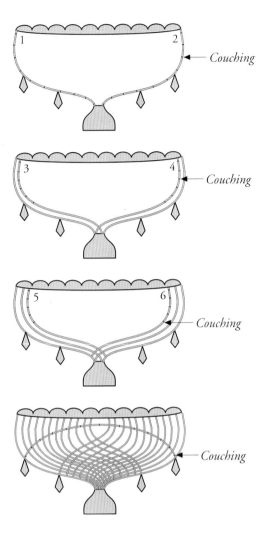

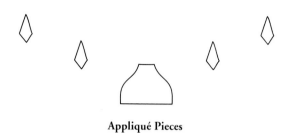

Appliqué Pieces

Stitches

(G) Bullion-tipped flower (page 23)

(D) Chain stitch rose (page 24)

(P) Couched loop flower (page 25)

Feather stitch (page 26)

Filled lazy daisy (page 26)

○ French knot (page 27)

Lazy daisy stitch (page 29)

Ribbon stitch (page 30)

Stem stitch (page 33)

Twisted chain stitch (page 34)

Outline Stitches

——··· Chain stitch (page 24)

—·—·— Stem stitch (page 33)

Placement and Embroidery Guide

ASSEMBLING AND FINISHING

Blocking

If you did not use a hoop when embroidering, the finished blocks may be slightly puckered. Blocking—gently washing and stretching each block—eliminates this problem. Blocking ensures that your measurements are accurate when you assemble your quilt top. Also, if your family and friends are anything like mine, the blocks have been touched by many people. All this handling may have soiled them. You probably won't want to wash the quilt when you're done, so this is a good time to clean the blocks.

Many of my students are concerned about colorfastness, but if you test your fabrics, floss, thread, and ribbon as recommended, you shouldn't have any problems.

You will need a dishpan, liquid dish soap, terry-cloth towel, straight pins, and mounting board. You can use a hair dryer if desired. (Blow-drying perks up the damp ribbon, making it look like new.) My mounting board is a 12" x 12" piece of cork glued to a plywood square. You can make a mounting board or use a cork bulletin board, ceiling tile, or even the carpet. Any surface will work so long as it is clean, will not be damaged by the wet fabric, and you can stick pins in it. Mark a grid on your mounting board so you can make sure the block is square.

1. Fill the dishpan with lukewarm water and a tiny bit of liquid dish soap. Gently swish a block around in the soapy water, then rinse thoroughly under cool, running tap water.
2. Using a folded terry-cloth towel, gently pat (don't wring) the block to remove excess water.
3. Lay the block face up on the mounting board and pin the four corners, stretching the block flat as you pin. Keep the block as square as possible. Place 3 to 4 pins along each side.

4. Allow the block to air-dry, or use a hair dryer.

Squaring the Blocks

It's time to trim the blocks to the finished size. This is your last chance to make sure the design is centered in the finished block. *Important:* Before trimming, refer to "Sashing" on pages 86–87 to determine the cut size.

You will need a piece of cardboard or template plastic, a ruler, marking pencil, craft scissors, and fabric scissors or rotary-cutting equipment.

1. To make a window template, mark and cut a 4" x 4" or 5" x 5" square (depending on the sashing method) from the center of the cardboard or template plastic.
2. Place a block right side up. Center the design in the window of the template, and mark a dot in each corner. *This is the finished block size, not the cutting lines.*
3. Using a ruler and marking pencil, add a ¼"-wide seam-allowance line to each side.
4. Using fabric scissors or rotary-cutting equipment, trim the blocks on the seam-allowance line.

Arranging the Blocks

No matter how many blocks you've made, arranging them can be intimidating. It helps to think about arranging your blocks as you choose your fabrics and threads and make the blocks, but we often avoid this step as long as possible. As I tell my students, part of the charm of antique Baltimore Album quilts is that each block is different and was meant to be that way. The inconsistency of pattern and color is part of the Baltimore Album style.

I do have a few hints for making the process more enjoyable. First, look at the quilts on pages 13–20 or at Baltimore Album quilts in other books. (See "Bibliography" on page 95.) Study the way other quilters set their blocks together. Focus on how they distributed pattern and color. Ask yourself why you like them or why you don't.

Now, lay your blocks in front of you and start arranging. Put your favorite block in the center and add blocks around it, trying to keep strong patterns evenly distributed. If possible, arrange your blocks on a design wall—a piece of flannel taped to a wall works fine. Step back for a better view. Squint your eyes and look at color, ignoring pattern. Are there blocks that stand out? These might look better in another area. If you don't have a design wall, look at your block arrangement upside down. (You will be less conscious of the individual patterns.) If all else fails, ask your family or the staff of a local quilt shop for help. They would probably be delighted.

When you are happy with the arrangement, make a list or place a numbered Post-It® note on each block.

Assembling the Quilt Top

Sew the blocks together by hand or machine. If you are assembling the blocks without sashing, follow these steps.

1. Stitch the blocks together in horizontal rows.
2. Gently press the seam allowances (don't smash the embroidery) in opposite directions from row to row.
3. Stitch the horizontal rows together, butting the seam allowances between the blocks.

SASHING

You can find antique Baltimore Album quilts with and without sashing. Sashing separates the quilt blocks into distinct, individual entities. Unfortunately, it can be a challenge to add sashing to a miniature quilt. Any misalignment in assembling the blocks seems magnified because of the small scale. Also, the border patterns in this book are based on finished blocks without sashing. If you add sashing, you will need to lengthen the borders to fit the center of your quilt. Instructions for lengthening the border patterns are provided on page 88.

This book includes two sashing methods: pieced and appliqué. You can make a traditional pieced sashing, sewing thin fabric strips between the blocks and rows, or you can appliqué folded fabric strips that mimic traditional sashing. For pieced sashing (at right), use ⅜"-wide finished strips. This width seems to be the easiest to manage and looks attractive.

For appliqué sashing (see page 87), trim the block slightly larger to accommodate the sashing. This method is easier and less risky than traditional sashing.

CHOOSING THE SASHING FABRIC

When choosing sashing fabric, look at small prints as well as solid colors. You can use a small geometric design to imitate traditional pieced sashing or to give the illusion of patchwork sashing.

Pieced Sashing

1. Refer to "Squaring the Blocks" on page 85. Trim your blocks to 4½" x 4½".
2. Cut 12 strips of fabric, each ⅞" x 45".
3. Beginning ½" from the top of the strip, sew a sashing strip to the right side of the first block. Trim the strip so it is ½" longer than the block. Stitch the second block to the sashing strip. Trim the strip even with the blocks.

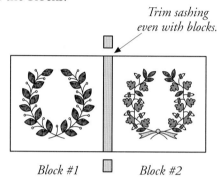

Trim sashing even with blocks.

Block #1   Block #2

4. Continue adding sashing strips between the blocks. Do not add a strip to the right side of the last block in each row.
5. Gently press the seam allowances in the same direction in each row.
6. Sew a sashing strip to the top and bottom of the first row. Trim the strips even with the blocks. Continue adding rows of blocks and strips and trimming.

7. Sew a sashing strip to the left and right sides of the quilt top. Trim the sashing strips even with the edges.

Appliqué Sashing

1. Refer to "Squaring the Blocks" on page 85. Trim your blocks to 5½" x 5½".
2. Stitch the blocks together in horizontal rows. Gently press the seam allowances in opposite directions from row to row.
3. Stitch the horizontal rows together, butting the seam allowances between the blocks.
4. Cut 1½" x 45" strips of sashing fabric along the straight of grain.
5. Fold the strips in half, then in half again as shown. Press the strips. Baste the center of each strip to hold it together.

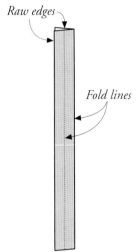

Raw edges

Fold lines

Fold strip in half, then in half again.

6. Center each sashing strip, raw edges down, on the seam lines and appliqué the folded edges. (For instructions on appliqué, see the "Bibliography" on page 95.) Appliqué the sashing strips to the outside edges of the quilt blocks after you add the borders.

Seam line

Adding the Borders

Borders provide continuity to the quilt as a whole. This book includes three border patterns in 4"-wide sections (excluding corner sections) to accommodate any number of blocks (see pages 92–94). Only the Grapevine border includes specific instructions for silk-ribbon embroidery. For the other borders, choose from the flowers you enjoyed in your blocks. Make sure to balance the colors and flower styles symmetrically around the border.

The Grapevine border mimics the Grapevine Wreath block (page 70). Unlike the other borders, the Grapevine border is not designed symmetrically. If you change the order of the pattern sections, you may need to add or subtract a leaf or grape cluster.

The Rose Garland border has an airy, delicate look. All the border sections are interchangeable. Notice that there are two sizes of leaves. Add buds in the stem intersections and distribute the silk-ribbon flowers and colors symmetrically around the border.

The Swag border is the most formal. Antique Baltimore Album quilts often include swags of red and green connected with tassels or clusters of flowers. When choosing colors for your swag, try to repeat the colors in your quilt top. This ties the color scheme together.

Before you mark your fabric, make a full-size border pattern for one side of your quilt. This makes transferring the border much easier.

MAKING A BORDER PATTERN FOR QUILTS WITHOUT SASHING

1. To calculate the length of the border for one side, multiply the number of blocks by 4.
2. Cut a piece of freezer paper 8" longer than the length calculated in step 1. Using a pencil, draw a straight line along one long side as shown.
3. Working from the left side, align the corner pattern with the pencil line and trace.
4. Continue tracing border sections A, B, and C, making sure the dotted lines match. After tracing section C, reverse the order and trace sections B and A and the corner. If you are using the Grapevine border, trace a mirror image from the center section.

MAKING A BORDER PATTERN FOR QUILTS WITH SASHING

Lengthen the border sections following these steps.

1. Measure the width of your quilt top across the center. Subtract ½" for outside seam allowances.
2. Cut a piece of freezer paper 8" longer than the length caluclated in step 1. Using a pencil, draw a straight line the same length as calculated in step 1. Mark the center of the pencil line as shown.
3. On separate pieces of paper, trace the sections you need, based on the number of blocks across your quilt. Do not include corners. Cut the sections along the center lines.

4. Using the center mark on the freezer paper as a guide, lay the cut sections along the length of the pencil line. Tape the sections to the freezer paper. If you are using the Grapevine border, trace a mirror image from the center mark.
5. Cut another piece of freezer paper the same length as in step 2. Lay this piece on top of the border pattern and trace. Fill the gaps in the pattern with stems, leaves, or flowers.
6. Add the corner sections to the ends.

CONSTRUCTING THE BORDERS

You will need border and appliqué fabric, paper-backed fusible web, a lead pencil or permanent-ink black marker, a marking pencil, an iron and ironing surface, and small embroidery scissors. Remember to trace the appliqué patterns on the *paper side* of the fusible web.

1. Using your freezer-paper pattern as a guide, cut 4 strips of border fabric approximately 1" larger than needed. Add ¼"-wide seam allowances around the border pattern.
2. Center 1 border strip over the pattern. Using a marking pencil, trace the design, including corners, on the fabric. Mark the outside edges so you can add seam allowances; trim the excess later. Repeat with another strip of fabric.
3. Center and trace the pattern on the remaining 2 strips, omitting the corner sections.

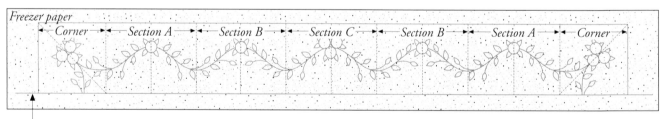

Freezer paper

← Corner → ← Section A → ← Section B → ← Section C → ← Section B → ← Section A → ← Corner →

Pencil line

Border without Sashing

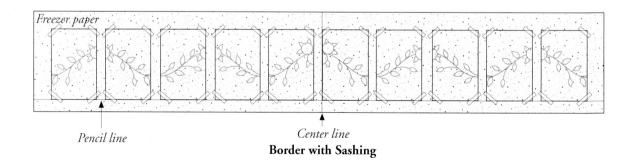

Freezer paper

Pencil line   *Center line*

Border with Sashing

4. Using a lead pencil, trace all the appliqué pieces on the paper side of the fusible web.

5. Cut the appliqué pieces apart. Referring to the manufacturer's instructions, fuse the section to the wrong side of the appliqué fabric. Repeat for each group of appliqué pieces.

6. Using a pair of small embroidery scissors, cut out the appliqué pieces.

7. Working as gently as possible, peel the paper backing from the appliqués.

8. Fuse the appliqué pieces to the border strips, following the pattern lines.

9. Trim each border strip to fit the quilt top. (Remember to add seam allowances to all 4 sides before cutting.)

10. Sew the borders without corner sections to the quilt top, then sew the borders with corner sections. Make sure the corners match up with the ends of the borders already attached.

11. Embroider as desired.

Marking the Quilting Design

When choosing a quilting design, keep in mind you will not want to quilt through the embroidered block designs. My favorite design is an allover diamond pattern as in Bernice Croushore's quilt "Remember Me" on page 13, but outlining each block also works well.

It is very important to use a removable marking pencil to mark the quilting design. I prefer chalk marking pencils; they usually wear off, or you can spritz them away with water. *Test your marking pencil before you begin and always mark very lightly.*

Layering and Basting

I like to use the same fabric for my quilt top and backing. Use a good-quality fabric to back your quilt. Remember, dark-colored backing fabric may show through the front of a light-colored quilt top. Choose an easy-to-quilt, low-loft batting.

1. Cut the backing fabric and batting 4" larger all around than the size of your quilt.

2. Lay the backing on a table or carpet, wrong side up. Using masking tape, fasten the backing to the surface. Make sure there aren't any puckers or folds in the fabric, but do not stretch the fabric out of shape.

3. Smooth the batting on top of the backing.

4. Lay the quilt top, right side up, on the batting, making sure the fabric grain is the same for the top and backing. Tape the corners of the quilt top to the work surface.

5. Beginning in the center, baste the layers. Work diagonally from corner to corner, then in a 4" grid.

Quilting

Some people have no problem quilting without a hoop, but I can't seem to keep my stitches neat and even unless I use a hoop. The silk-ribbon embroidery in these Miniature Baltimore Album quilts would be crushed in a traditional hoop, so I adapted a set of artist's stretcher bars. These are usually available at craft- or art-supply stores. Purchase a set the same size as your quilt top, approximately 27" x 27". (If you purchase a larger set, you won't be able to reach the center of the quilt top.) You will also need 12 large binder clips—the sort used to hold papers together—available at office-supply stores.

Assemble the stretcher bars into a square frame, then lay the basted quilt over the frame. Using the binder clips, clamp the quilt to the frame. As you work, move the binder clips out of your way. This method also works well for larger quilts, especially those with delicate dimensional appliqué.

You also need quilting thread, needles (Betweens), and a thimble. Use the smallest needle you are comfortable with.

1. Cut an 18"-long piece of quilting thread and thread the needle with a single strand. Make a small knot at one end. Insert the needle in the top layer of the quilt, a slight distance from where you want to start stitching, then pull the needle out where you want to begin stitching. Gently pull the thread until the knot pops through the fabric and into the batting.

2. Using a running stitch, take small, even stitches through all 3 layers of the quilt as shown. Rock the needle up and down, placing 3 to 4 stitches on your needle at once. Place your other hand under the quilt so you can feel the needle point with each stitch.

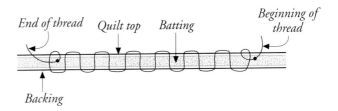

End of thread   Quilt top   Batting   Beginning of thread

Backing

3. To end a row of quilting, make a small knot next to the last stitch. Backstitch through the layers, about a needle length, and gently pull on the thread to pop the knot into the batting. Carefully trim the thread even with the quilt top.

Adding a Sleeve

Unless you decide to frame your quilt, you will want to attach a sleeve for hanging.

1. Cut a 6"- to 8"-wide strip of fabric 1" shorter than the width of the quilt. Turn the short ends under ½" twice and stitch.
2. Fold the strip in half lengthwise, wrong sides together, and baste the raw edges to the top edge of the quilt back. This edge will be stitched when the binding is attached.

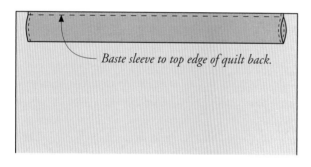

Baste sleeve to top edge of quilt back.

3. After attaching the binding, blindstitch the bottom of the sleeve to the quilt. Push the bottom of the sleeve up slightly before stitching. This provides a little give so the hanging rod does not put strain on the quilt.

Binding

Make binding from bias or straight-grain fabric strips.

1. For a French double-fold binding, cut 2½"-wide strips of fabric. Cut enough strips to go around the outside perimeter of the quilt, plus 10" for seams and mitered corners. For example, if your quilt is 27" x 27", cut 118" of binding fabric.
2. Sew strips, right sides together, as shown to make one long piece of binding. Press the seams open.

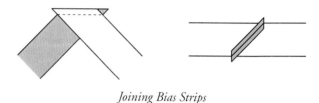

Joining Bias Strips

Joining Straight-Cut Strips

3. Fold the binding in half lengthwise, wrong sides together, and press.
4. Turn under one end of the strip at a 45° angle and press. This eliminates bulk where the two ends meet.
5. Trim batting and backing even with the quilt top.
6. Using a ⅜"-wide seam allowance, stitch the binding to the front of the quilt, aligning the raw edges of the binding and the edge of the quilt. At the corners, stop and backstitch ⅜" from the edge as shown. Trim the thread.

⅜" ►| |◄—

Binding strip

Quilt top

7. Rotate the quilt 90° so you will be stitching down the next side. Fold the binding up and away from the quilt.

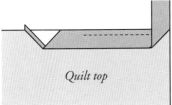

8. Fold the binding back onto itself, parallel with the edge of the quilt. Start stitching ⅜" from the corner, backstitching at the edge.

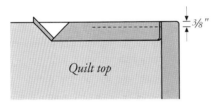

9. Continue stitching around the quilt. When you reach the beginning of the binding, overlap the ends about 1". Trim at a 45° angle. Tuck the raw end into the fold and finish the seam.

10. Fold the binding to the back of the quilt, covering the seam, and blindstitch in place. Blindstitch the mitered corners.

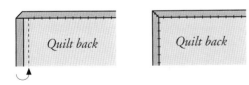

Signing Your Quilt

Be sure to sign and date your quilt, either on the back or in one of the front blocks. Include as much information as possible: your name, the name of the quilt, date or dates you worked on the quilt, and your location. If you are making a label for the back, include the recipient's name, if it's a gift, or other information about the making of the quilt. Imagine how much more we would know about Baltimore Album quilts and their makers if they had made these sorts of labels!

Grapevine Border

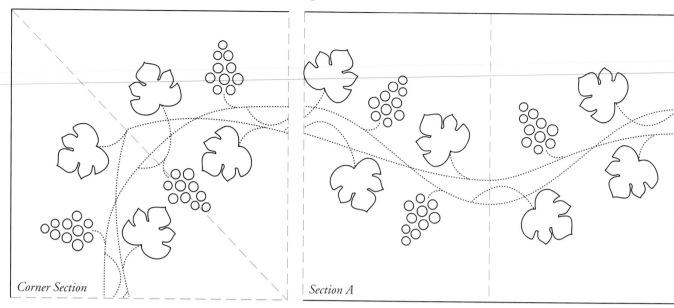

Corner Section

Section A

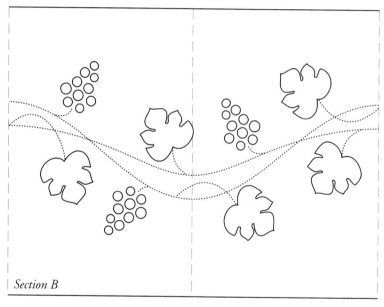

Section B

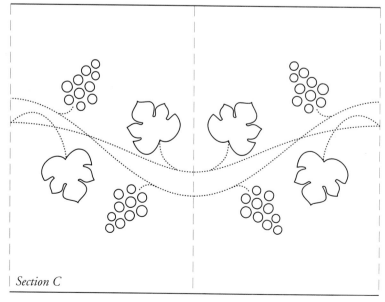

Section C

Rose Garland Border

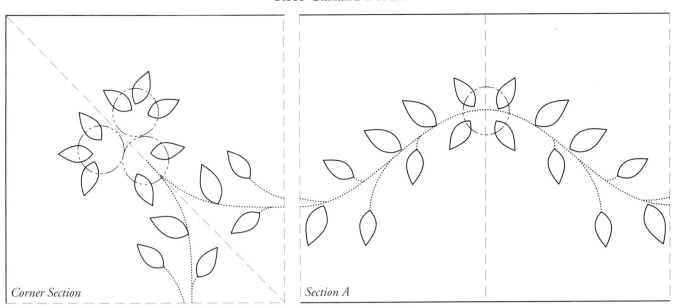

Corner Section

Section A

Section B

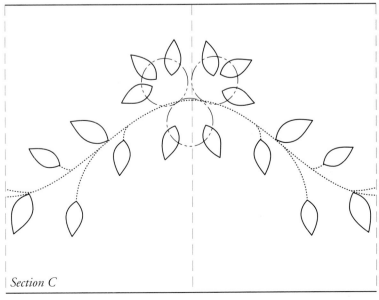

Section C

Swag Border

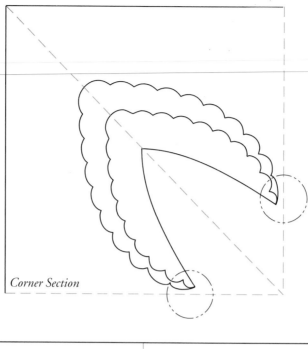

Corner Section

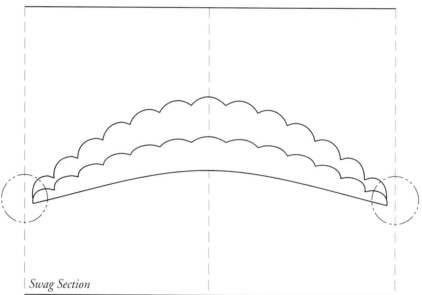

Swag Section

RESOURCES

Hand-Dyed Silk Ribbon
Jenifer Buechel
Box 118
3567 Mountainview Drive
West Mifflin, PA 15122
Eighty-four variegated shades of silk ribbon in a variety of widths as well as braids. Send $2 for a color card and ordering information.

Clotilde, Inc.
1909 SW First Avenue
Fort Lauderdale, FL 33315-2100
1-800-772-2891
Sewing accessories, from needles and scissors to ribbons and threads. Call for a free catalog.

Bernadine's Needle Art Catalog
PO Box 41
Department BA
Arthur, IL 61911
Send $2 for a catalog full of flosses and threads to embellish your needlework.

Dover Publications, Inc.
180 Varick Street
New York, NY 10014
Victorian clip art and calligraphy design books. Write for a free catalog.

BIBLIOGRAPHY

Appliqué

Linker, Sue. *Sunbonnet Sue All Through the Year.* Bothell, Wash.: That Patchwork Place, Inc., 1994.

Embroidery

Heazlewood, Merrilyn. *Silk Ribbon Embroidery Roses.* Hobart, Australia: Little Stitches, 1992.
———. *One Hundred Embroidery Stitches.* New York: Coats and Clark, 1964.

Montano, Judith Baker. *The Art of Silk Ribbon Embroidery.* Lafayette, Calif.: C & T Publishing, 1993.
Sienkiewicz, Elly. *Baltimore Beauties and Beyond: Studies in Classic Album Quilt Appliqué, Volume 1.* Lafayette, Calif.: C & T Publishing, 1989.

Quilting

Hanson, Joan, and Mary Hickey. *The Joy of Quilting.* Bothell, Wash.: That Patchwork Place, Inc., 1994.

MEET THE AUTHOR

Marilyn Ingalls, Ingalls' Images

Born and raised in Pittsburgh, Pennsylvania, Jenifer Buechel has a full house with her husband, Ron; two teenagers, Heather and Ryan; two old dogs; and two young cats. She has been quilting for about fourteen years and has tried more crafts, sewing, and needle-arts projects than she can remember. After winning several quilting awards, she began teaching at a local quilt shop. Since then, she's been designing original quilts and class projects. She teaches at a number of local shops.

INDEX OF STITCHES